WHAT OTH

Judy's story is really every person's story since we all have "handicaps." Her narrative sparkles with creativity and hope. As they have learned to receive gifts from God the Creator and Redeemer, Judy and her family have experienced His Majesty. Theirs is an adventure in grace from which we all may learn His limitless mercies through our brokenness. Judy's story affirms the Divine alchemy that turns stones into gold, silver and precious stones in each of our lives.

Elaine Stedman
Wife of Pastor Ray Stedman, www.raystedman.org

One amazing woman – that's Judy Squier. After 14 years, I still remember the moment I met her – impacted not by her missing legs but her radiant, overflowing joy. This is a woman we all can learn from. Judy's life shows clearly that no matter the missing pieces – seen or unseen – God has a victory for each of us. Thank you, Judy for sharing your wisdom!

Barbara Curtis
Author, www.Mommylife.net

There is no more compelling argument for the existence of God than someone who points joyfully to her Creator in spite of severe disabilities. It makes no worldly sense. Judy honestly shares her struggles of a life without legs. Her greatest limitations became God's most effective vehicle to show His Majesty through her daily trials. As her friend, Judy has taught me how God is glorified as we come face to face with our own brokenness (oftentimes not visible) and find Him to be all sufficient.

Mary Schaller
President of Q Place, www.qplace.com

Love to Letha
and Leeza

His Majesty in Brokenness

Judy Squier

JUDY SQUIER

www.judysquier.com

You are loved by
His Majesty and me!

Self-published by Judy Squier.
www.judysquier.com

Cover & interior design by Naphtalie Squier (www.scatterjoydesigns.com)

Squier, Judy
His Majesty in Brokenness / by Judy Squier
ISBN-10: 1453677143
EAN-13: 9781453677148

Printed in the United States of America

DEDICATED TO DAVID,
my beloved husband,
whose sacrificial love has been
my ticket to
an extraordinary life.

Contents

In Appreciation

I'm thanking You, God, from a full heart,
I'm writing the book on your wonders.
I'm whistling, laughing and jumping for joy;
I'm singing your song, High God.

Psalm 9:1-2 MSG

Thank you to my extended family,
who believed in me when I didn't.

A special thank you to Tina,
my sister and soul mate.

Thank you to my husband and our children,
for your love and patience
as we have lived many of these stories together.

A special thank you to daughter Naphtalie,
my graphic designer extraordinaire.

Thank you to fellow writers
Pat, Cathy, Kathy, Katie, and Barb
Your expertise gave my writing wings.

Thank you also to Marcia, LJ, Becky,
Rachel, Sydna, Christie, Suzanne, Eloise,
Diana, Marilee and Marge
for your legs that carried me to the finish line.

And a special thanks to Gunther and Gretel Grace,
my faithful dachsies,
whose licks rescusitated me when needed.

Preface

Born without complete legs, I watched others have all the fun. The whole time I believed that those with legs had "No worries, Mate." As I watched them walk, run, climb stairs, and dance, I was certain they were living the life I was missing. As I wore my orthopedic shoes, I had no idea what God could do with broken me. As I coveted other kids' physical adeptness, their social calendars, and their seeming satisfaction in their own skin, I remained clueless that they indeed shared my condition – a missing "something" in their lives.

It took decades before I realized the truth:

- You can have long, strong legs but no one wants you on their team.
- You can have intact, beautiful bodies but be unhappy with what you see in the mirror.
- You can look perfectly whole but be filled with gaping holes.

Each one of us is broken in some way. For some it's visible; for others it's hidden. It may be acne or a terminal illness. It could be an absent parent or a passive spouse. Many walk around with learning problems, emotional instability, or social challenges. Others covet freedom from abuse, from personal addictions, or from financial insecurity. Life's pain seems unending.

And yet in life's inevitable pain the unexpected can happen. It did for me. While I was concluding that life was passing me by, a full and fulfilling life was in the making. Through an invisible strength, a unique, anchored life was taking shape. Not all of a sudden, but little by little – glimpses of good appeared. Proof that God exists. And cares.

St. Augustine alluded to a God who has much to give us but is hindered because our arms are full. Could it be that in order to bless us, God needs such unlikely elements as missing legs? Empty arms? A broken heart? A dysfunctional family? The nightmare of addiction? Could it be that these are fertile soil for holy ground, a place where we can turn back and see His footprints?

His Majesty in Brokenness shares stories of my life lived in intimate relationship with God, thanks to some everyday missing pieces – not just legs, but self-sufficiency, courage, and a social life. Could it be that the very absence of these ingredients provided the stage for God to perform the impossible?

And here's an even more important question: What's missing in your life? Normalcy? Freedom from fear? Good health? Marketable skills? A paycheck? Self-control? Stability? Answers? Whether you see Him or not, God has pitched

His tent in that very wasteland. He says:

Be astonished! Wonder!
Because I am doing something in your days –
you would not believe if you were told.

Habakkuk 1:5 NASB

I pray that as you read my stories you will contemplate God's presence in your own life, His Majesty crafting the places of your brokenness into His unique masterpiece called YOU!

CHAPTER 1
His Majesty in Adversity

People with disabilities are God's best visual aids
to demonstrate Who He really is.
His power shows up best in weakness
and who by the world's standards
is weaker than the mentally and physically disabled?
As the world watches these people persevere.
They live, love, trust and obey Him.
Eventually the world is forced to say:
How great their God must be to inspire this type of loyalty.[1]

Joni Eareckson Tada

CELEBRATION ON HOLD

The day of my birth was not a celebration. In fact, I have a hunch my birth announcement had an invisible PS that was obvious to everyone: "In lieu of balloons, bring a hankie."

My midnight arrival was like a cold shower to the unsuspecting obstetrician. With no speech prepared for such a tragedy my dad recollects the doctor blurting out, "Your daughter is going to live, I am sorry to say."

Mom remembers that she waited three days before the nurses brought me to her. Expecting the worst, she was surprised to find me "capable, not a vegetable" when I didn't just wiggle but turned over in the nervous nurse's arms. Evidence that there was life and strength. "And your big brown eyes," Mom swears, "jumped out and wrapped themselves around my heart."

Leaving Geneva Hospital in upstate New York that cold day in March, no pink blanket could hide the fact that I had severe birth defects – a webbed left hand and two undeveloped legs with no thighs or knees and a total of five toes instead of ten. Proximal femoral focal deficiency (PFFD), future hospital records would read.

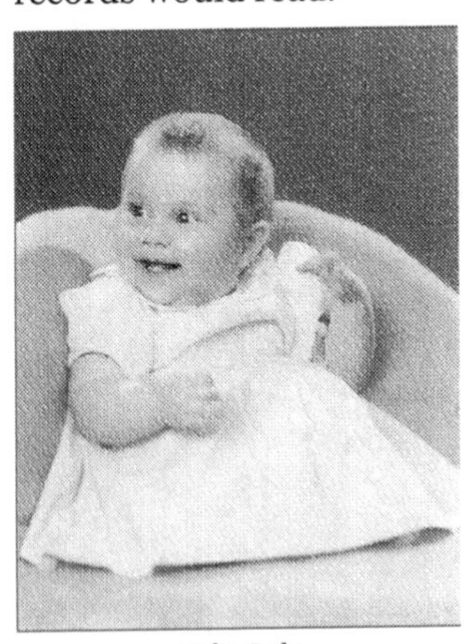

Baby Judy

Mom and Dad said my five pound, six ounce incomplete body seemed light when contrasted with the unending questions weighing heavy on their broken hearts: Will our baby die? How can we take care of her? If she lives, is she educable? How can she ever enjoy life?

Too busy to stay stuck on the questions, my family dug in their heels. Changing diaper after diaper on a baby with webbed feet cured the initial shock. People's dead silence in place of "What a beautiful baby!" made mom madder than a hornet, but ceased to surprise her.

Tears, hard work, laughter, faith, failure, and success filled the years ahead. Countless doctors' appointments, operations,

Dad, Mom, Sister Tina and Little Judy

trips to the brace man, and eventual placement in special education were added to the usual stuff of "growing-up," filling each week to the fullest. But the life-changing event we had all held our breaths for came when I was ten. At Shriners Hospital in Chicago I underwent corrective surgery and traded my deformed footies for stumps and my metal stilts for artificial limbs. Standing tall for the first time in my life, my willow wood legs and I walked the long haul – I mean hospital corridor – the day I was discharged.

My legs and I entered domains no one ever dreamed possible. A military ball, driving a car, summer jobs at a camp, college, and a sorority filled and thrilled my young adult years. And the prize after six years at the University of Illinois was an M.S. degree in Speech Pathology the same month I received my Mrs. Degree and became Mrs. David Squier.

These milestones became midget-sized compared to the births of my three daughters. God more than compensated for everything I had missed, times three. Vicariously, I have walked, run, jumped rope, rollerbladed and played soccer. Sitting at Emily's piano recital, watching her nimble ten fingers make Michael Card's *El Shaddai* dance on the keyboard,

I wondered if the concert auditorium would shake as shivers of celebration danced up and down my spine. I've gloried in the back flips and front walk-overs as Betsy's and Naphtalie's limber legs have carried me the length of the gymnasium.

Somewhere in the journey, at different times for each of us, the hundreds of family and friends have exchanged the no-longer-needed hankies for helium balloons. Unbeknownst to us, God made my life a celebration. Together we had learned that disability is a potential delivery room for the extraordinary, the unprecedented, the inconceivable. And in the process, His Majesty companioned with me every step of the way, even when I didn't know He was there.

What About You?

How easy it is to get bogged down by life's trials. We trudge on and on, never expecting a happy ending. I can tell I still wear some scabs from my early years when I hear Pastor Floyd's Sunday morning reminder to the congregation: "God always answers prayer and He's never late." Invariably something deep inside of me retorts: "But He's never early either."

Whether early, on time, or seemingly late, God's surprise is that we are strengthened through our trials. Adversity, while we feel it is enfeebling us, is actually empowering us.

What is breaking you today? It may be something you were born with or born without. It may be someone you can't live with or live without. Don't lose hope. You are not alone. God is there. He's been there all along.

Keep your eyes peeled. His Majesty is throwing a party and the guest of honor is YOU. The banquet hall location will be your brokenness redeemed.

P.S. No hankies needed.

Chapter 2
His Majesty in Loneliness

God is a circle whose center is everywhere and circumference is nowhere.

Empedocles

The Empty Chair

My first memory of life is at age two when I was lying in a crib viewing the world through metal rails. I felt totally alone even though I was surrounded by a dozen other patient-filled cribs in the girls' ward at Chicago's Shriners Hospital. This hospitalization would be the first of many to mend my broken body.

To this day I remember the empty chair beside my crib, a constant reminder that I was alone. In the 1940s and '50s, Shriners restricted parents' visits to a few hours on Sunday afternoons. Even on surgery day, the chair remained empty. Moms and dads, not permitted to be present, received a post card to inform them that surgery had happened and the patient was doing well. No one ever questioned the forced separation. We followed the rules, eagerly anticipating the results. To this day I will greet a Shriner with a huge thank you and a hug for mending broken me.

Shriners Hospital played a major role in my growing up years until I outgrew their life-changing services when I turned eighteen. My childhood friends were nurses rather than the kids in my neighborhood. The names Miss Nancy, Miss Bonnie and Miss Sue appeared in my little red daily diary intermingled with tales of hospital school during the week. Saturday nights were the highlight of the week, watching *Hit Parade* on TV with a ward full of girlfriends. Somehow trips to the green surgery room and the inevitable appointment with the black ether mask were camouflaged by the camaraderie we shared.

My longest stay at Shriners lasted six months. Admitted in January 1955, just before my tenth birthday, I underwent surgery to prepare my severely deformed lower limbs to wear artificial limbs. By mid June, I stood tall in my first of seven sets of artificial limbs over a span of fifty years.

Later in life my young daughters would accompany me to the *legman* near our home outside San Francisco. Enroute we'd drive past a Shriners Hospital whose red-brick building looked just like my hospital in the Midwest. I'd invariably say, "That's Mama's hospital. I stayed there when I was a little girl. Surgeries were a drag, but we still had lots of fun."

"Mom, can we go there?" they would beg.

They didn't have the ticket for those hospitals. Their bodies were intact. But many years later, one of those little girls grew up and went to work in a group home for severely disabled kids. On a day off that grown daughter and I visited one of her special charges at Stanford Hospital. There in the hallway stood a crib exactly like my crib at Shriners. I was immediately transported back to the forties and fifties, to a time when family and friends feared life would pass me by. To a time when I already knew that life was passing me by. To a time of hopelessness, loneliness, and pain.

"Emily, that's the kind of crib I had as a little girl in the hospital!" I exclaimed as we passed it in the hospital corridor.

My emotions flashed back half a century to the crippled child I was as I relived the questions that had loomed then: Would I ever have a life? Would I ever go to college or marry? Surely I'd never be a mother... But wait – beside me stood my daughter! Suddenly the spoken and unspoken questions received their answers. Suddenly God performed an unscheduled surgery, replacing early hopelessness with amazement, as I connected the dots and saw the rest of the story. I was living the future that no one could have anticipated. I had gone to college, married, and I was a mother three times over.

It was then that the hospital crib changed from a symbol of suffering and loneliness to proof of God's faithfulness. And more. Tommy Tyson, a Methodist evangelist once said, "There are parts of me that haven't even heard of Jesus yet." My early memories of hospitalizations were void of Jesus. I couldn't see Him as my broken body peered through the metal rails into the sterile hospital room. But when He and I met in that hospital corridor decades later the reality hit: He had been my round-the-clock visitor at Shriners. Indeed He had faithfully occupied the empty chair beside my crib.

What About You?

What symbol in your life reeks of unfulfilled longings? Despite garages and and rented storage units bursting at their seams, we could all make a long list of unmet needs – needs that more things can't satisfy. Maybe you have a ring finger that never donned a wedding band. Maybe your family gathering is minus a loved one. Or maybe you, like me, have an empty chair beside your bed of pain.

Life has taught me that empty places set the stage for us to discover a God who cares. Whether we see Him or not, His Majesty companions with us round-the-clock. We are never alone. And there's more. Our unfulfilled longings can actually become blessings in disguise which, like a magnet, draw us and attach us to the only One who satisfies.

Lord, may our suffering not be wasted. Open our eyes to see Your comforting presence especially for those times when we feel totally alone.

Chapter 3
His Majesty in Hopelessness

When you say a situation is hopeless,
you are slamming the door in the face of God.

Charles L. Allen

Star Light Star Bright

My sister Tina and I had a ritual we'd perform during our Sunday night rides home from Grandma's. Two little girls, Tina was seven, I was four, tucked in the back seat of Dad's '48 Chevy, were on a mission to improve our destinies.

"You two warm enough back there?" Dad would ask as he guided his four door sedan through the light snow flurries on the country road outside Naperville, Illinois. Mom, wrapped in her chinchilla coat, fretted, "I hope this doesn't turn into a blizzard."

Bundled in toasty woolen blankets, leaning against opposite car doors, Tina and I laughed as we anticipated our Sunday night highlight. Unknowingly, Dad provided the needed signal as our family putt-putted past a lone road sign. "We're on the home stretch now, girls. Have a good snooze."

His words triggered our song:

Star light, star bright, the first star I see tonight;
I wish I may, I wish I might have the wish I wish tonight. [2]

With our wishing chant completed, our hands excitedly rubbed the moisture from the car's fogged side windows – up, down, right, left – a peek hole was cleared. Simultaneously, but worlds apart, our pixie noses and rosy cheeks pressed against the ice cold window glass.

Sister Tina and Judy

Two sets of brown eyes peered longingly up into the night sky, straining, seeking. In the stillness our little hearts hung big dreams on distant stars.

With ten chilled toes wiggling excitedly inside two galoshes, Tina fixed her gaze on the black sky's brightest star. Confidently, she mouthed her checklist: *Handsome. Strong. Popular with enough money to take me to the movies on Friday nights.*

Completing her wish, she turned to kneel in the middle of the worn gray seat. Moving Dad's fedora hat aside, her gloved pointer finger stretched to the car's rear window where she drew a sturdy heart. Inside went her initials: CRR.

Across the dark divide of the car's back seat, I sat. With my five, not ten, chilled toes wiggling inside my high top orthopedic shoes, I hesitantly selected the faintest star in that night's winter sky. With no expectations, I mouthed a wish

I was afraid to voice, a dream I felt unworthy of dreaming: *Anybody to marry me someday... pretty please,* I whispered into the darkness.

Familiar with the sequence of the wishing game, I awkwardly turned and reached up to the back window. With no knees, I propped myself on two stubs for legs. Moving dad's hat with my mitten-clad webbed hand, I drew a crooked heart minus my initials.

None of us could see the road beyond the weak headlights that black wintry night. But God, whose light brightens our darkness, surely smiled knowing the plans He had for me were good with a future and a hope. (See Jeremiah 29:11 NASB) His hope would most definitely suffice for my lack of hope. And He would teach me to trust in Him, the God of hopeless cases.

What About You?

What are you afraid to hope for? Growing up, each one of us has someone or something missing from our life. God knows our heartaches even when we're unable to put our initials on them. He shows up calling to us in our pain.

I remember God showing up when my family and I had lost hope during my wilderness-adolescent years. Romans 12:12 NEB jumped out at us during our morning devotions. Mom and I held on to it for dear life: *Let hope keep you joyful. In trouble stand firm. Persist in prayer.* Weak-kneed, we'd steady ourselves by reciting that verse as a reminder to entrust my bleak future to the God of hope.

Will you join me in hope? His Majesty invites you to slam the door on hopelessness. How? By replacing your wish list with a prayer list so that faith, not fate, can bring you through.

Chapter 4
His Majesty in Loss of Vision

To love the unlovely makes God visible.

Author Unknown

The Love of the Father

My father loved a challenge. Given the choice, he'd choose an impossible task over an easy-fix any day. His friends all knew Christian Rieder was the champion of challenges with a specialty in restoring broken things. They'd seen the cinder heap behind the parsonage he transformed into a rose garden. They'd marveled at the rain-ruined, three-legged table he'd brought home from the side of the road – now a mahogany drop leaf treasure standing in his living room. Dad was a craftsman of the highest order. With God's grace, Rev. Rieder conquered the insurmountable until one day he knew he'd met his match.

I know his heart broke the day I was born. Until his dying day, he replayed Dr. Duel's chilling words, "Your daughter's going to live, I'm sorry to say." Some fathers shut down when called to parent a child with severe problems. My father went the other direction. Mom said I became his mission in life. He lived and breathed giving Judy Ann the best life possible.

He carried me on his shoulders when I didn't grow. He adapted tricycles and bicycles and eventually automobiles when I was old enough to drive. He made sure I had a chance to try horseback riding, ice skating, dancing, and tree climbing – all the things my older sister Tina did. He taught me the compensatory skill of public speaking, and when I turned thirteen, he launched my speaking career – inspirational talks about learning to walk with artificial limbs. He pried the door open so I could attend a Big Ten university, though the state social worker declared I was not college material. And I could have sworn I heard his heart singing Handel's *Hallelujah Chorus* as he walked me down the aisle to give me in marriage to David Squier. His mission was accomplished. I was launched.

Knowing that my father's love plucked me out of the rubble gives me goose bumps. He believed in me when I couldn't believe in myself. He cheered me on until I stood on my own two feet. He made sure I mastered walking, while his love taught me that I'd never walk alone. Dad at my side somehow translated into a Heavenly Father at my side. Like the Heavenly Father, my father knew the plans that he had for me. They were plans for good, carefully crafted to give me a future and a hope. And he never gave up even when I wanted to.

We all knew Dad didn't like down-and-outers. Surely the prize went to the swift. But wait a minute, I wasn't swift. He'd fix that. Can-do Judy was shaped by his vision and determination coupled with Edgar Guest's motivational poems, which we memorized together. Our all-time favorite was:

It Couldn't Be Done

Somebody said that it couldn't be done,
But he with a chuckle replied
That "maybe it couldn't," but he would be one
Who wouldn't say so till he'd tried.
So he buckled right in with the trace of a grin
On his face. If he worried he hid it.
He started to sing as he tackled the thing
That couldn't be done, and he did it.

Somebody scoffed, "Oh, you'll never do that;
At least no one ever has done it;"
But he took off his coat and he took off his hat,
And the first thing we knew he'd begun it.
With a lift of his chin and a bit of a grin,
Without any doubting or quiddit,
He started to sing as he tackled the thing
That couldn't be done, and he did it.

There are thousands to tell you it cannot be done,
There are thousands to prophesy failure;
There are thousands to point out to you, one by one,
The dangers that wait to assail you.
But just buckle in with a bit of a grin,
Just take off your coat and go to it;
Just start to sing as you tackle the thing
That "cannot be done," and you'll do it. [3]

Quitting was never an option, nor was discouragement. I remember how disappointed Dad was when post-partum depression downed his cheerful Judy after daughter number three was born. My gloom cloud was compounded by his unexpected cloudburst, "I'm deeply troubled, Judy. You've lost your song!"

Dad's *never quit* rule stuck with me long after his death so much so that I anticipated his disappointment when at age 61, I traded my artificial limbs for a full-time wheelchair. Disappointing my dad even posthumously was very painful, even when my prosthetist Bill dittoed my decision and applauded my *seldom-seen* determination that had kept me marching for half a century – well beyond the norm.

No dad ever loved a child more than my daddy loved me. He knew my life would be hard so he *buckled us both in with a bit of a grin,* and made me an overcomer with no room for wimpin' or whinin'. Dad put legs and feet to Paul's words in II Corinthians 4:8 NASB: *We are afflicted in every way but not crushed, perplexed but not despairing...*

Reverend Christian Rieder (Dad) & Judy

I am certain my father joined the huge crowd of men of faith in the grandstands of Hebrews 12:1 taking his well-earned front row seat reserved for the *more than conquerors* crowd. His love saw invisible value in the broken things and people of this world. He plucked us out of the reject pile, rehabilitated what was missing, and created a masterpiece. Isn't that what our Heavenly Father does?

What About You?

Who in your life shaped you into the person you are today? If not a parent, maybe it was a grandparent? For some it's a Sunday School teacher, or a classroom teacher or a coach. Who laid the groundwork on which God could add His finishing work?

Possibly the person of greatest influence did everything wrong and you carry lifelong scars. The good news is that in Christ nothing is wasted. God's specialty is to take what we label *the end of the world* and use it to save our souls. Redemption means He uses what we say is killing us – to give us Life.

I can still hear Dad's benedictions at the end of a Sunday service, which he recited for anyone on earth who had lost their vision. This one stands out in my memory:

Now may the God of peace Himself sanctify
you entirely; and may your spirit and soul
and body be preserved complete,
without blame at the coming of our Lord Jesus Christ.
Faithful is He who calls you,
and He also will bring it to pass.

I Thessalonians 5:23-24 NASB

CHAPTER 5
His Majesty in Exclusion

When you come to the end of all you know,
you must believe one of two things –
you will find earth on which to stand,
or you will be given wings.

Author Unknown

LIVING ON THE SIDELINES

I felt so isolated during my elementary school years, huddled in a segregated group of special education classmates. Yes, we became family, but deep down we all knew we were bench warmers on the sidelines of life.

Year after year a station wagon transported me to a classroom miles away from home while my sister walked three blocks to the neighborhood school – the school that denied me entrance because I was an insurance risk. Morton High School's Orthopedic Department was my small world for eight years. Day after day, my life was lived in a handful of out-of-the-way rooms inside a brick building that filled a city block.

There wasn't much cross-over between us and the thousand plus able-bodied high schoolers, except for one brave soul. Freshman Geri Jacobson ventured into our closed community and welcomed us into hers. Sent by God, Geri volunteered in our classroom during the week and invited me to her home on weekends for sleepovers. She gave me a corsage on my birthday. She taught me how to crack my gum and wolf whistle. We laugh at such things now, but the truth is Geri's friendship plucked me off the sidelines.

My exit from the orthopedic classroom came with my eighth grade graduation at age thirteen. A graduation never looked so sparse, but, hey, it was a glorious moment for three thankful graduates who could now attend regular high school classes. That day in June 1958, was the first day I'd seen Calvin in a necktie. Marguerite and I wore dresses beautiful enough for a debutante ball and sported our best-ever hair-dos.

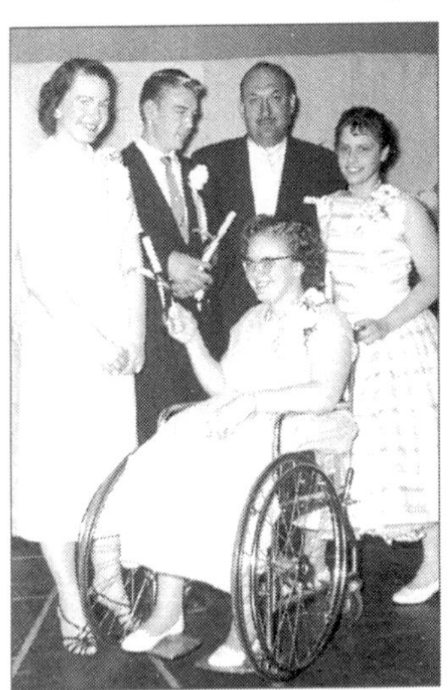

Eighth-grade graduation, Teacher Miss Horky, Calvin, Superintendent, Judy and Marguerite in wheelchair

We didn't march in to Sir Edward Elgar's *Pomp and Circumstance.* Marching was out of our league. Marguerite was in a wheelchair and I stood not-too-securely on my first set of artificial limbs. Instead our trio sang *You'll Never Walk Alone,* a song selected by our teacher Miss Horky, who wanted to launch us into life's future on a brave note. We'd rehearsed it for weeks. The song was a perfect fit for our lives. We'd walked through the winds and rains of exclusion. We hoped our future would be better than our past.

Eighth grade graduation day was a big moment for our parents too, who knew life's milestones could also be mile high hurdles. Sitting proud that day, I doubt that any of them realized they held the key to our futures. More than ever, warriors would be needed – parent advocates who dared question and challenge the system that would define our destiny.

High school was a shocker until my junior year when I finally learned the ropes. But my senior year, I hit a locked door to higher education when the State Department of Vocational Rehabilitation's social worker decided I was not college material. My parents fought it. Dad talked to our councilman who did some investigating. We were told that the decision was in the hands of a psychiatrist. I drove Calvin and myself to a medical office in downtown Chicago. The psychiatrist took note of that, then he talked with me for a brief ten minutes. His conclusion, "All this girl needs is a chance." His words unlocked the door and off I went. I attended the University of Illinois for six years and left with a master's degree.

I can count on my three-fingered left hand the number of us who made it to college. Out of a dozen or so, one classmate would become an engineer, another a scientist and I would become a speech pathologist. The rest of the kids were stuck in time. Several married but the majority spent the rest of their lives in the town they grew up in, many remaining at home with mom and dad.

Looking back, I'd say my early education was stunted. Our

teacher did her best but no educator could single-handedly bring such a heterogeneous group of students grades three through eight to their fullest potential. The system, defining individuals by their disabilities alone, was as handicapped as we were. Humans and our man-made programs try their best but they can only reach so far. That's why there has to be more, something beyond our human limitations. Someone.

I didn't see it then but I can see Him now, warming the bench with me. He knew it was temporary. He knew my seemingly endless boredom would be replaced by a life filled with productivity and excitement. He had big plans for the little girl with a stunted body to go beyond a stunted educational program to become a college graduate. I never would have dreamed it possible.

WHAT ABOUT YOU?

And you? Do you feel like a bench warmer on the fringe of life? Or maybe it breaks your heart to see a loved one stuck year after year, seemingly on the road to no where?

To those of us who feel like a caterpillar trapped inside a cocoon, I pass on the encouragement my Aunt Ruth gave me during my cocoon years. Her gift of a wall hanging contains a pressed butterfly with some dried flowers and these words by an unknown source:

What the caterpillar calls the end of the world
the Creator calls a butterfly.

So dear caterpillar, grow strong during your waiting period. Become informed. Become an advocate. Join readily available support groups. And most importantly, don't quit before the happy ending. Your week-after-week cocoon captivity is not a waste. It is merely the waiting room before you get your wings.

Chapter 6
His Majesty in Solitude

God doesn't believe in the easy way.

James Agee

A Twenty-Four-Karat Miracle

Sorting through the glitter of one flowering teenager, I craved the razzle-dazzle of a fun-packed life – invitations galore, sock hops, sleepovers, the sparkle of after-school clubs, summer bashes with "best friends" at Riverview, Chicago's Amusement Park. Hey, a few drops of water at the local pool when the noon temperature hit a sizzling 100 degrees would have satisfied me.

I watched the early morning whirlwind and beheld what was left behind, layers of chic clothes piled sky high on Grandma's rumpled patchwork quilt. The day's rejects after the wild pursuit of today's "perfect outfit."

My ears rang in synchrony with the incessant telephone, which I prayed brought a call for me. But each time my hopeful hello sustained a prick of rejection as I passed the still warm receiver to our family's favorite daughter.

Deep down I realized the dazzle was counterfeit, not

Judy and Sister Tina

genuine gold. I knew for a fact our Georgian brick house west of Chicago did not house Morton High School's homecoming queen. I knew, too, that the fashion plate who stepped through the front door had not been voted America's best dressed coed. She was just another teenager with her own well-hidden insecurities and acne under control.

But even baubles can tantalize the impoverished. To me, a cute coed donning a cashmere cardigan with a pleated skirt and burgundy penny loafers complete with a shiny copper was enviable. A group of newly blossoming teenage girls, sweet-smelling like an English garden of lavender, was admirable. And a Friday night pep rally with a football game followed by a hot fudge sundae at Seneca's was to die for!

Yet at age thirteen, I was but a spectator drooling over my sister's sweet sixteen life. Not just her little sis, but her *crippled sis,* I sat and watched from my reserved seat on the eyelet pillow at the top of her bed, bracing myself for the twister. Like clockwork, I then moved downstairs and repositioned myself at the right corner of Mom's olive green couch, the spot closest to the front door to greet my sister's friends. When the excitement and the teenagers departed, my life began. In place of friends and fun, I had a pair of artificial limbs standing in my closet challenging me to get up and walk. With an empty calendar, my life was unhurried. Uncluttered. Unevent-filled. Solitary. Idle. With an occasional activity mixed in.

One of my favorite pastimes was to sit at the upright piano. With coaxing, my eight fingers would peck out a tune in Dad's old hymnal as I sang along in my one octave range. In the stillness, my soul discovered a still life. A simple contentment inside my solitude. With nothing and no one to distract or to anesthetize, I made the acquaintance of the One who companions with the lonely and the left out. He sat beside me on the piano bench so I was no longer alone. He walked with me through the solitary years. In the fellowship of His presence I discovered self-worth. Purpose. Truth.

Day after day, my family weathered my desert years. My mother's heart silently ached as she loved one child who had and one who had not. My father's creative talents were stretched beyond human capacity as he labored to transform a wall flower into a rose. My sister pushed the Judy-filled stroller to the public pool even on sweltering summer days when she'd rather not – the hallmark of a saint. And I marched on day in and day out in the company of boredom and monotony.

But while I was feeling as solitary as an oyster, an amazing thing happened. I didn't see it then but I know it now. Hour upon empty hour, weekend after boring weekend, God was with me in the pit. No black hole is too deep or dark for His Majesty. He crawls down, cohabits with us, and brings us out, not tarnished and torn, but refined and together we come forth as GOLD. Truly a twenty-four-karat miracle.

Now that we two sisters are grown, the rest of the story emerges. Come to find out, as I watched my sister who had it all, she was watching me. She saw in me something that glistened as real gold – a joy in the wasteland and a hidden strength for the journey. Life had proven to her that popularity doesn't satisfy and a full calendar can leave one empty. As an adult, she exchanged her hollow trappings for the only thing that satisfies – a relationship with my ever-present Friend, who waits patiently for us to trade life's trinkets for fulfillment in Him.

What About You?

Does it feel like life is passing you by? Does it look as if others are having all the fun? An old Chinese proverb says: *What seems to be may not be what is and what is may not be what seems to be.* How easily we humans can be deceived by what dazzles in front of our eyes. Someone else's engagement ring or promotion or winning ticket from the lottery. Don't be fooled. Glitz and glitter are often faux.

Pure gold requires testing. Human suffering can test the best of us, but in God's economy, pain and loss can provide surprising rewards. Our cries for relief do not go unheard. His Majesty's specialty is to redeem the years that the locusts have eaten. Ultimately He will replace the ashes of our life with bouquets of roses, the news of gloom with messages of joy, and in place of our languid spirit He will give us a praising heart. (See Isaiah 61:3 MSG)

In Him, dear reader, your wasteland is not wasted. In your poverty God wants to mine a wealth this world knows nothing of. The apostle Peter, who was certain his life was over after denying Christ three times, concludes: *Pure gold put in the fire comes out of it proved pure; genuine faith put through this suffering comes out proved genuine. When Jesus wraps this all up, it's your faith, not your gold, that God will have on display as evidence of his victory.* I Peter 1:7 MSG Herein lies the ultimate twenty-four-karat miracle.

Chapter 7
His Majesty in the Unexpected

No eye has seen, no ear has heard,
and no mind has imagined
what God has prepared
for those who love him..

I Corinthians 2:9 NLT

A Change of Heart

"God Bless the Bride. God Bless the Groom," chimed the bell from high up in the little country church's white clapboard belfry that joy-filled day in June 1952.

A hundred heads turned so a hundred pairs of eyes could watch the dark oak doors swing open. *Here Comes the Bride* was surely the next number to be played in the humble piano's prenuptial medley.

Pestering the eager expectancy, like the summer fly that whizzed from pew to pew, was a latecomer. Definitely not the bride. Trying to be inconspicuous, the preacher's daughter hustled in and took a seat in the front row. The seven-year-old stood tall – sort of – aided by metal-stilts that gave a bit of height to her midget-sized stature. But the congregation knew the truth. Under the pink and white seersucker sundress were malformed legs. Inside the orthopedic shoes were deformed feet, missing toes. And inside the white cotton gloves were eight fingers instead of ten.

"She was born that way," a local guest whispered to an out-of-towner who gawked at the child without meaning to be disrespectful. Yet, as always, Judy's confident countenance, buckteeth and all, prompted a sanctuary full of smiles. Bittersweet smiles. Grateful smiles from parents who uttered a thank you to the God who had given them healthy, fully formed children who had a chance for marriage and a normal life.

But there was one guest who didn't smile. A freckled-faced nine-year-old boy with aquamarine eyes thought to himself the truth that no one else dared to utter, "Pity the man who marries her."

Many a bride came and went through that vintage doorway during the lifetime of this little church in America's heartland. But the bell seemed to peal its loudest and proudest in June 1968 as folks from as far east as New York and as far west as California gathered to witness the wedding of the preacher's daughter.

Standing tall in her "they look so real" artificial legs, she resembled a princess bride in her white dotted Swiss gown with its six-foot-long train. Radiating from behind the European lace veil was her perfect smile. Teardrops of wonder dampened cheeks, and one hundred souls clapped their hands as a hundred pairs of eyes followed the bride step-by-step down the starched ivory wedding carpet. With one pearl-sequined glove secure on her preacher-father's strong arm, Judy Ann leaned her other hand on her daisy-decked cane. Arm in arm, father and daughter threw invisible kisses to a thankful mother in the front pew.

Judy and David's Wedding Day

As the *Wedding March* ended, the hundred pairs of eyes contemplated the handsome groom, now a grown lad whose freckles were no more. His aquamarine eyes were riveted on his bride and his heart, changed by the One who had created both bride and groom, sang the new song he had engraved in her engagement ring: *There are many fine women in this world, but you are the best of them all.* Proverbs 31:29 NLT

My wedding was truly the surprise of the century. But equally astounding was the discovery that my groom-child was tucked in bed less than fifty miles from the road where my sister and I played our Sunday night wishing game as little girls. While Tina's wish oozed with confidence, my timid wish indeed fell short. But faltering as it was, our sovereign God overshadowed it by writing my initials on this little boy's heart.

David and I started dating in college just before he graduated and moved 2,000 miles away. After three years of daily letter writing, Wednesday and Sunday phone calls and four visits per year, the dream I never dared to dream happened. Following 1,000 love letters each plus 300 phone calls between Illinois and California, David Squier popped the question. He proposed on Palm Sunday, and we were married sixty-four days later on June 8, 1968. That was the day my family and friends celebrated a God who grants even wimpy wishes and makes even impossible dreams come true.

What About You?

Humanly, you and I fall short in one way or another, wishing we could wear stilts to give us height physically, intellectually, emotionally or socially. Often we end up excluded from life's givens, aching for the life we never expect to enjoy. Hope can run short before it's over.

If only we could hear His Majesty's endearing words – *My little one, just wait 'til you see what I have planned for you. You're going to love it!*

Have His Majesty's plans for good intercepted what's missing or broken in your life yet? If not, don't lose hope. He's the Master of the unexpected.

Chapter 8
His Majesty in Relinquishment

What is undoable on my own becomes
unstoppable to God in me. [4]

John Ortberg

The Birth of Emily

My chiseled-in-cement response was automatic when anyone dared to ask the question, "Are you and David going to have children?" With conviction that grew stronger every year, I'd retort, "There are two things in life I never want to do: have a root canal or have a baby."

I'd heard horror stories about root canals and I believed my fears of childbearing to be well-founded. I remember Mom's wise words when I was in elementary school, "Judy, don't you do it! Don't ever have kids!" Hers was more than the usual concern. She had miscarried her first pregnancy, had had an appendectomy six months into her pregnancy with my sister, and was bedridden during much of her pregnancy with me. Then, I arrived with a birth defect. My poor mom!

Curiosity alone led David and me to a genetic counselor three years into our marriage. When told we had a fifty percent chance our offspring might bear my disability, the cement dried on my decision. Add to that my misgivings about the physical aspects of child rearing plus my off-the-charts fear of labor and delivery, I decided I'd pass on motherhood.

We can always "prove" that we are right, but is the Lord convinced? says King Solomon in Proverbs 16:2 TLB. In our case God obviously wasn't convinced by my seemingly good arguments. He began to engineer His plan ten years into our marriage during a heart to heart talk with my sister Tina. "Judy, you're well into your thirties now. Any chance you and David might still have children?"

My *maybe so* was a shocker to both of us. But what would David's response be? Tina and I found him in his office at the other end of our house and with great caution broached what had become a touchy subject. Surely this was the 100th time he and I had talked about kids. Always we'd been out of synch. If one of us wavered with a surprising *maybe we should,* the other's strong as steel *No Way!* reinforced our resolve. But this day in wide-eyed wonder, we both agreed it might be nice to have at least one child. So began our about-face.

My change of heart was validated by two close girlfriends who were first time mamas. Both reported problem-free pregnancies and they'd both survived delivery. The prize for all of us was their adorable, healthy babies. My boss, Cindy, ecstatic about my new interest in motherhood, proceeded to telephone the public library to gather information. I turned crimson as she queried the librarian, "When exactly in a woman's ovulation cycle is pregnancy most likely to occur?" She upped the volume on the librarian's answer – obviously wanting me to take note of the answer.

My other friend, Marilee, had been preaching to me for three years, "Judy, you'd be a great mother." Despite my repeated arguments that I would be a lousy candidate for pregnancy, labor, delivery, and motherhood, I was catching her vision.

Our final concern was resolved when David and I scheduled an appointment for a second genetic study. Unable to find my birth defect in his textbook of hereditary disorders, the new geneticist concluded we had only a one half of one percent (0.5%) chance that our baby would bear my birth defect. Our risk was no greater than anyone else's.

With these developments, David and I made a choice to move in the direction of a family. My age – I was nearing thirty five – plus my ten years on the birth control pill caused us some anxiety. But this didn't lessen our God-given enthusiasm and newborn desire to have children.

Feeling somewhat nauseated on New Year's morning, 1979, I managed to attend church, though I was sure I had the flu. God knew differently and made certain I got a copy of the inspirational thought on the front of the bulletin: *Am I hanging on to something old at the expense of taking hold of something new in Christ?* became the litmus paper to keep my attitude in check through the uncharted territory ahead.

The thrill of learning that the New Year's tummy ache was morning sickness and indeed, I was pregnant, was coupled with many fears: Would motherhood be as fulfilling as my career in speech pathology? Was I willing to be bedridden for three-fourths of a year, if necessary? Who was I kidding? Of course I couldn't survive the pain of childbirth! I was far from a woman-of-faith, but God delights in honesty. Given a surrendered heart, there's no limit to His outpouring of miracles. Day by day, He showed up as I let go of the old and reached for the something new in Christ:

- My pregnancy was without complication. I felt like I was at the prime of my life and David said I never looked better. My major complaints were an insatiable craving for McDonald's hamburgers, then tacos, then ice cream and finally Clausen's Dill pickles – plus some minor gall bladder problems that were reduced with a change of diet.
- My weight gain totaled twelve pounds, not enough to throw off my balance wearing my artificial limbs. I was on my feet and, in fact, in the office the day before delivery.
- Gradually my fear of giving up a career I was good at and entering the unknown was countered with a growing confidence that God was trustworthy. Indeed He was asking me to let go of an old life that I knew was good, so I could enter a new life that would be His best.
- And finally, what I dreaded for decades, the labor and delivery, came and went so fast I nearly missed it. Following my three hours of labor at

home, ten minutes in the ambulance and three minutes in the Emergency Room, Emily Beth entered time. All five pounds, six ounces of her. Her beaming dad didn't recognize her gender until he had carefully scrutinized her whole body with ten fingers, long legs, knees, feet and ten toes. Thank You, Lord!

Soon after her arrival, God unveiled the uniqueness of Emily Beth's birth date:

- On August 14, 1965, thanks to my Aunt Ginny, I experienced a new birth when I asked Jesus Christ into my life as Savior and Lord. (My life is a classic example of how one can grow up in the church and come away with religion not a relationship.)
- On August 14, 1978, one year earlier to the day, David and I were dining at Emlee's Restaurant in Carmel, California and made the decision to call our first daughter Emily.
- And on this August 14, 1979, our Heavenly Father gave us Emily, a cooing and kicking memorial stone reminding us that His specialty is to walk us head on into our fears, teaching us that in Him there is nothing to fear.

And how special to discover later that the name Emily means *diligent one*. Surely God had built into her special abilities to be Mama's helper should the Squier Family have additional memorial stones – which we did. Within five years, Emily was joined by two sisters, Elizabeth Christine and Naphtalie Joy – three daughters to fill their dad's quiver.

My friend Marilee gave words to the miracle, "Judy, how good God is! You were born with no legs and now you have six good legs."

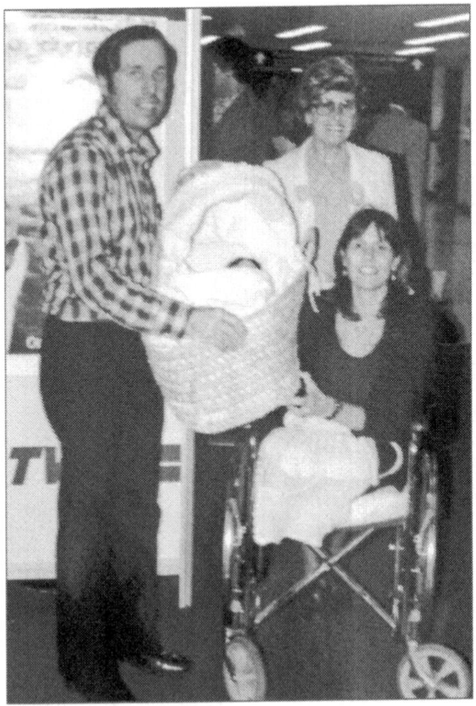

David, Judy and Baby Emily welcoming Grandma Rieder at SF Airport

WHAT ABOUT YOU?

Are you holding on to something old at the expense of taking hold of something new in Christ? We humans maintain a tight grip on our fears, beliefs and life plans even when they sabotage His Majesty's plans for our life. If God could change my *no* to motherhood into the *yes* of becoming the mother of three wonderful daughters, He can also bulldoze your brick wall of fear of the unknown.

But God's bulldozer requires a surrendered heart. I know that's easier said than done. Let me share a secret. Each time my *No way Jose* digs in its stubborn heels, I grab for verse Psalm 119: 32 in my Amplified Bible: *I will not merely walk but run the way of Your commandments when You give me a heart that is willing.*

Yes, God can change mule-headed hearts into hearts that are willing. God gently leads us in the direction of His perfect plan for our lives by situating our heart's desire in the middle of our Not Me's. He's a pro at transforming a stalwart NEVER into a faith-filled yes!

One step at a time, hanging on for dear life to His Majesty, can you go forward into your *never?* That's where fulfillment is found. There is no greater joy than finding God's Masterpiece in what you almost missed.

Chapter 9

His Majesty in the Strain

Alone we can do so little;
together we can do so much.

Helen Keller

Motherhood: A Team Approach

Deep down I knew that caring for my children would involve more than my fair share of miracles. Not only would my family have to pitch in and become masters of teamwork, but God would also have to pitch in more than in the average home. Let's face it. Because of my artificial limbs and wheelchair, motherhood would literally be a balancing act. I would need to discover an equilibrium between my limitations and my responsibilities, and pray for His Majesty to make up the difference.

Obviously my becoming a mom was not an uninformed or whimsical decision. David and I spent a decade asking ourselves the hard questions. But we didn't know if we had the answers until the arrival of Emily. I was thrilled to find myself able to walk holding my baby, although this was only possible as each one adapted to me. Early on, don't ask me how, as the muscle tone in their necks developed, each one intuitively leaned her chin into my left shoulder, arching her back, as I steadied her torso with my left hand while leaning on my cane with my right.

I learned the practicality of dressing our infant daughters in bib overalls, so when they were on a blanket on the floor, I'd roll them onto their tummies and pick them up by the suspenders. Reaching the milestone of standing, they learned quickly that my extended forearm against their waist was a signal to lean over so I could swoop them up with one arm. Giving mom a hand kicked in soon after they learned to walk and could understand directions like "Bring mama the keys" or "Go see if sister's awake." Before long they could even help *me* dress. What a magical age when a toddler loves to help.

Emily, Betsy and Naphtalie assisting Mom

It's been said that necessity is the mother of invention. This axiom proved true as this disabled mom witnessed the precocious bonanza of my children's untapped potential. Long after the novelty of being mama's super helper had worn off, our children continued to make the physical contributions needed for me to become the best mom I could be. The girls and I developed unique systems, bringing new meaning to the word cooperation. Chasing after a younger, free spirited sibling, carrying in the groceries, running up a flight of stairs as mom's delivery service to someone's front door, and eventually getting mom's wheelchair in and out of the car became early tasks for three young girls.

Did this stifle their freedom or leave a negative mark? Quite the contrary. Being helpful is inherent to our human nature. I was reminded of the propensity of a two-year-old to help several years ago when I found myself trapped at the dead end of an overstuffed aisle in a department store. Inadvertently, my wheelchair had bumped a small box onto the floor behind me. Pre cell phones, I thought "Lord, I'm trapped here. Help!" Suddenly I heard a little tike behind me whispering words to accompany actions he'd been taught, "Put this back, put this back," he repeated half a dozen times as he picked up the shoe box returning it to the perfect spot on the shelf. "So young to be my hero," I said out loud as my mind flashed back to the dynamics that had kept our family on a forward roll.

Yes, the Squier girls were team players from the start. At three Naphtalie, our youngest, was expected to empty the dishwasher. She took her job seriously. A little too seriously,

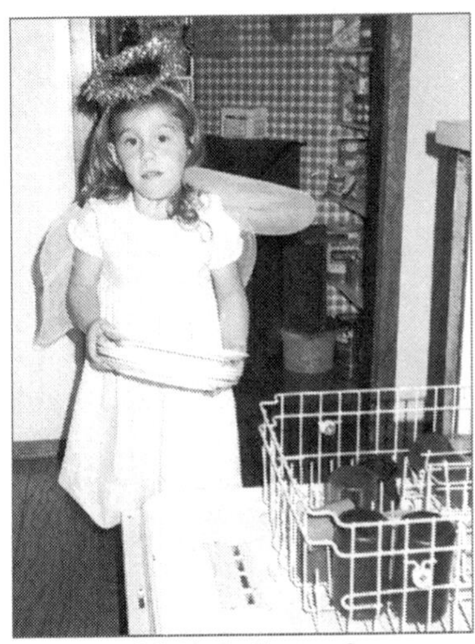
Little Naphtalie at work

we discovered when she voiced her anxiety about entering kindergarten, "I don't want to go to school. You can't manage without me, Mom."

For middle daughter Betsy, heavy-duty participation proved to have a hidden perk. Her PE coach expressed amazement when this ten-year-old broke the national record for chin ups. The explanation was obvious when we told him Betsy's job was to carry in the milk. Having seen her mom model efficiency, her style was to transport two gallons in one hand so she could make it in one trip.

Emily was the one who testified to His Majesty's masterpiece, thanks to our family's brokenness. She was the daughter who at age two had watched me crash to the ground outside the library when my left prosthetic leg broke. Her siren-like screams brought a passerby to the rescue. First he carried her, then he carried me to the car. Then mother and daughter made an emergency trip to the *legman,* where I was glued back together. Mama got fixed, but traumatized Emily refused to let me hold her or hug her for a month afterwards for fear I'd break again. That daughter, as a freshman, passionate about the sanctity of life, won first place in the high school speech contest. The conclusion of Emily's speech was a personal standing ovation for me, the mother who daily wondered if my daughters would be handicapped by my handicap:

> *My mother is one of the most important people in my life and in many others. Because of her faith in God she has reached out and touched many lives with her amazing stories of how God works in her life. How He changed her pain and suffering as a child to glory and happiness as an adult. Every single person on this earth was put in this world for a purpose. Each life is sacred and specially made by God. My mother has proven that. Even though she was born with less than most people have, she can still be all that she can be, which is a lot!*

What About You?

What feels exhaustingly impossible for you right now? What situation causes you to wring your hands as you reach the sorry conclusion, "I can't do this!"

When I felt like I was in over my head, whether in the midst of motherhood or a mega house remodel, my friend Linda would throw me the life line as she joyfully reminded me of God's infinite creativity, "Judy, our God has a 1,000 creative solutions for what seems impossible to you right now."

Can you let go of whatever is overwhelming you? Hand it over to God. Tap into His infinite resources, His 1,000 ideas. And receive supernatural strength from His affirmation, *You're doing an amazing job. Allow Me to companion with you and we'll cross the finish line together.*

Chapter 10

His Majesty in the Uphill Climb

Be not forgetful to entertain strangers:
for thereby some have entertained angels unawares.

Hebrews 13:2 KJV

Angel Unaware

You'd better believe our announcement "Judy's pregnant!" was headliner news. Family, friends and strangers held their collective breath until receiving the report that we were the proud parents of a healthy baby girl. God heard lots of prayers for my early months of motherhood.

The instant I realized that Emily and I could actually manage the dailies was the instant David and I wanted more children. When I sailed through the next pregnancy, labor, and delivery of our precious second daughter Betsy, sure enough we were ready for one more. Most people said, "Don't do it!" but I'd lived for ten years with my own unfounded "Don't do it," so I was unstoppable. We were ready to add one more arrow to David's quiver, having become firm believers in the truths of Psalm 127:3 and 5 NASB: *Behold children are a gift of the Lord; the fruit of the womb is a reward.... How blessed is the man whose quiver is full of them.*

But by the third pregnancy, I began to have days I was sure I had bitten off more than I could chew. One of them was when I was eight months pregnant with Naphtalie and running late for an OB appointment. Wearily, I loaded my wheelchair into our adapted van, strapped the two girls into their car seats and hoisted myself into the driver's seat. I felt like a mother elephant.

Disappointed to see the handicapped parking spots by the hospital entrance full, I had no choice but to park down the hill. Turning off the ignition, I sat for a spell doubting my strength to make it to the top of that morning's literal mountain.

That's when I noticed him – a middle-aged man standing in front of my van. Our eyes met. He smiled and walked to my door. I rolled down the window and heard his heaven-sent words, "What do I do to help?"

Too fatigued to ask him how he knew I needed help, I talked him through the unloading routine. First, he got out my wheelchair. Next he helped me into it. He carefully lifted two-year-old Betsy onto my lap and watched as four-year-old Emily walked to her spot and grabbed hold of the armrest. I rested as he pushed my chair up the incline, through the automatic doors, and around the corner to the elevator. After he pressed the elevator button, I turned to thank him, but no one was there.

I proceeded to the doctor's appointment, then to the grocery store. The girls and I had lunch and took naps. I cooked and served dinner, cleaned up the kitchen, and put baby Betsy to bed.

When all was done, Emily and I snuggled side-by-side in our favorite rocker. Reviewing our day, I suddenly remembered the man who had come to our rescue. "How did he know we needed help?" I asked more to myself than to Emily.

That's when it hit me – the reality that had been gently germinating all day! I remembered God's promise to send angels to help us – angels unaware.

In awe, I looked over at my daughter and announced what was no longer a silent hunch:

You met an angel today, Emily.

What About You?

Are you battle weary with no idea how to make it up to the top of your day's mountain? Do you need someone else's energy to offer you a boost? Though your circumstances may shout, "The cheese stands alone," your needs do not go unnoticed to God. Help is on the way.

Sure we've all had times when we were going down for the count and no angel appeared. We limped along, seemingly on our own. But even those times are not wasted. Spiritual faith muscles were being strengthened and we managed by His invisible grace. Don't be bitter. Don't let that steal the wonder. Keep your eyes peeled. When you most need it and least expect it, God will show up with skin on.

My experience tells me to not expect Him to send a regal angel with wings and a flowing robe. To date, most of His heaven-sent rescuers have been dressed as simple earthlings with big hearts, giving a hand to someone God and they saw in need. The day my van died in the middle of a busy intersection, my angel appeared with a cigarette hanging out of his mouth. Not what I'd expect, but I do believe I detected a halo atop his matted gray hair. Even a toddler has saved my day more than once. And maybe you've seen a four-legged guardian angel with a tail – leading a blind woman across eight lanes of rush hour traffic. Service dogs always make me shout, "Angel in disguise."

And don't forget, you too can be someone's angel in disguise. My 90-year-old friend, Esther, says this simple prayer before her travels, "Lord, use me to help someone in distress." He's never failed her yet as He strategically places her in situations where her what-can-I-do-to-help prayer convinces others that God hears and answers both spoken and unspoken SOS prayers for aid.

Proverbs 3:27 MSG exhorts us: *Never walk away from someone who deserves help; your hand is God's Hand for that person.* Let's pray that God opens our eyes to golden opportunities at airports, grocery stores, family reunions, wherever we may be – to be His Majesty's hands and feet to that someone who is waiting for Him to save their day.

CHAPTER 11

His Majesty in the Already But Not Yet

Energize the limp hands, strengthen the rubbery knees, tell fearful souls, "Courage! Take heart! God is here, right here, on his way to put things right and redress all wrongs. He's on his way! He'll save you!" Blind eyes will be opened, deaf ears unstopped, lame men and women will leap like deer, the voiceless break into song, springs of water will burst out in the wilderness, streams flow in the desert.

Isaiah 35:3-6 MSG

MY REVERIE

Gingerly, my agile legs, leaping like a sure-footed deer carried me through brittle autumn ground cover to the creek bed. Longing, craving, arriving, rejoicing. I stepped into the cool water, trickling over moss-covered rocks. My ten toes splashed with the glee of my once little toddlers, who, but yesterday, it seems, entered this same creek for the first time. Today my big toe explored cautiously, wondering if it might meet a crawdad, but finding instead a thousand and one jelly bellies – pebbles in creek language. My frolicking knees kicked up sprays of water while the dusty buckeye leaves thanked them for a bath.

Carefree legs running, jumping, carrying me. Feet standing, stepping, touching. Heels and soles savoring and sending good reports to a mind that has yearned for just this.

The raucous song of my three dogs jolted me out of my reverie. The German shepherd howled bass, the beagle barked baritone and the chipmunk-sized dachshund sang tenor. I moved my wheelchair closer to the deck's edge, straining to see what visitor might be at my creek in the twilight-cooling of this Indian summer day.

Could it be the three fawns responding to their instinctive clocks, lapping droplets of life-giving water at eventide? In the shadows, I imagined three Iroquois squaws, chestnut colored, kneeling, drinking clear, unpolluted water many moons ago when my acre was their acre.

Ah, tonight it's my coming of age daughters who had exchanged the day's strain and sweat for the stream's coolness. Laughingly, lazily, leisurely they ascended the steep bank, climbing toward the deck where I sat. I heard refreshing tales of water fights and crawdads and my comfortably wet girls one by one by one presented me with their love token – a wet jelly belly deposited into my treasure jar.

In my mind I walked in the creek tonight. My willow wood legs with artificial feet and no toes frolicked, explored, and experienced my dear friend, Los Trancos Creek. Vicariously, I tasted its refreshment. This twilight, it was my reverie.

But, one day in heaven's glory, it will be a reality. In utter reverence I will walk, skip and dance in the river of the Water of Life. As my ten toes take a dive, I will shout:

Goodbye dependable wheelchair.
Goodbye strong willow wood legs.
You served me well, but please, excuse me.
I've got creek-walking to catch up on.

What About You?

I've never been one to daydream. Wishing upon a star was a real stretch for me. Yes, I admit I've been afraid to be disappointed. But believing God's promises is totally different from fantasizing or crossing one's fingers.

God's Word tells us that blind eyes *will* be opened, the lame *will* leap like deer and the voiceless *will* break into song. That tells me that one day my blind niece, Christie, will look upon the faces of her daughters she's yet to see. That means my remark to the prosthetist crafting my fourth set of artificial limbs was true, "In heaven, you'll be out of a job." And for those of you with no voice secondary to physical or emotional traumas – eternity will be graced with your song.

If that's true, what are we waiting for? Why not whoop it up now if our brokenness is *a momentary, light affliction producing for us an eternal weight of glory?* II Corinthians 4:17 NASB

Bring on the balloons. Let your party begin as we lap up the reality of God's already but not yet.

Chapter 12
His Majesty in the Struggle

If you think you are standing strong, be careful not to fall. The temptations in your life are no different from what others experience. And God is faithful. He will not allow the temptation to be more than you can stand. When you are tempted, he will show you a way out so that you can endure.

I Corinthians 10:12-13 NLT

Wrestlings

Wrestling matches can break out in unexpected places, even at home in a laundry room, even while one is still in pajamas. I know. I was caught off guard one morning as I was dressing. As usual my shoes and socks were already on. They stay on day and night, whether I'm in my artificial limbs or my legs are off duty in the closet.

Having hoisted myself from my wheelchair into my "I'm ready when you are" prostheses, absent-mindedly I pulled my worn stump sock through the suction socket to create the vacuum that held my legs on. A no-brain job. Scanning the Formica counter, my eyes stopped at an old family photo. Actually it was new to me. My self-image gasped and I uttered out loud, "That's me!" My prostheses and I stood there

– stunned, numbed, bummed!

Strange how we can live with ourselves all of our lives but not really see ourselves. Maybe it's self-preservation. But what do ya' bet "good lookers" see themselves all day long. However, if your body were my body, I think you'd have learned to close your eyes.

I'm not sure why I'd never seen this picture before. Mom said it came from Aunt Pauline's collection, which Aunt Edna inherited, which ultimately my parents ended up with. Going through Mom's things at Thanksgiving, I had found three treasure-filled boxes peppered with a mish-mash of papers.

How exactly that photo ended up on my laundry room counter – right where I take my legs off and put my legs on – beats me. But seeing it, I suddenly felt sucked into a wrestling match and the opponent was a pro. I hadn't experienced that "dark, dirty" feeling for decades. Instantly, I felt my prosthetic knees buckling as I remembered the condemner's fatal, all too familiar refrain, "Nothing good can come out of you."

Once again I became the six-year-old in the faded photo:

Yes, I stood lopsided.
Yes, they were my deformed footies.
Yes, they were my "much too long" arms.
Yes, I did run on all fours, like an orangutan.
Yes, you're right.
I should never have worn that bathing suit.
Swimsuits are revealing, even the old
fashioned one-piecers.
Yes, it's true, everything showed.

Standing with one foot in the laundry room and one footie in the fifties, trying not to fall off balance, amidst the purr of the washer and the hum of the dryer, I heard myself speak the unspeakable, "God, You made me like this. What a dirty trick! What a dirty trick!"

Succumbing, truly I was, to that deadly grip of shame, I felt myself being pinned to an all-too-familiar mat. But did I have time for this? My motherly responsibilities jolted me up from the mat and out of the ring. Three daughters were waiting in the kitchen. It was lunch time. "Time out," I uttered to my arch enemy, "You wait here, I'll be right back."

Hurrying to the kitchen – I don't even remember dressing – it was a relief to see Betsy, my fifteen-year-old, tossing the Caesar salad. I dropped the photo on the table. Simultaneously dropping my "not to worry" mother image, I wailed in desperation, "How can I believe that God loves me? Look at this."

Seventeen-year-old Emily, standing close by, looked at the picture. With sincerity, bless her heart, she lovingly remarked, "Mom, you only think that because it's you. I think you were cute."

"You do?" I said, wanting to believe her words and feeling better already.

Sitting at the kitchen nook, eating bagel bites and Betsy's Caesar salad I looked ahead from the photo and back over my life. Reviewing the truth in silence, my mind loudly stated my case:

My children have seen me at my worst.
Legs on. Legs off.
Walking like a penguin.
Helpless on the ground,
needing help up after a fall.
They've tied my shoes and helped me put on my pants. Never have they expressed embarrassment about me being their mom.

Yes, my daughters' unconditional love had plucked me out of the wrestling ring into a new arena called Acceptance. They had proven me worthy of a heavyweight title.

"No match today," I thought with a new confidence.

In my heart, I imagined sending my third-born into the laundry room's wrestling ring to take care of business. Naphtalie's melodic name, taken from the Old Testament means *wrestler*. Yes, Naphtalie, tall and slender on strong legs, could take my place. Her life alone could silence any claim that "Nothing good could come out of me."

Rising to clean up the kitchen, I shouted, "Match canceled!"

WHAT ABOUT YOU?

What do you wrestle with?

Show me one human being who hasn't wrestled with self-acceptance. Fashion models, homecoming queens, Rhodes scholars, average Joes, CEOs, NFL superstars – no one is exempt. None of us would turn down the opportunity if God said, "Pick one thing you don't like about yourself and I'll change it." If you're at all like me, you might even say, "Lord, may I pick ten things?"

It's been said the condemner whispers to nonbelievers, "You're wonderful. You don't need a Savior." But to believers he bellows, "Look at what a loser you are!"

Simon Peter warns us, *Keep a cool head. Stay alert. The devil is poised to pounce and would like nothing better than to catch you napping. Keep your guard up.* I Peter 5:8 MSG I like the New American Standard version too: *Keep alert. Your adversary, the devil prowls about like a roaring lion seeking someone to devour.*

For those of us who wrestle with negative thoughts and self-condemnation, I pass on a few nuggets from Max Lucado:

If God had a refrigerator, your picture would be on it.
If he had a wallet, your photo would be in it.

He sends you flowers every spring
and a sunrise every morning.
Whenever you want to talk, he'll listen.
He can live anywhere in the universe,
And he chose your heart.
And the Christmas gift He sent you in Bethlehem?
He's crazy about you.[5]

If that's true, and it is, it's time we pull the plug on the condemner's lies. The truth is, no matter how you look in the photo, God loves you. He puts you on the front page of His family album. His love isn't based on how you look or how you perform. God's love changes not, no matter how you assess your worth. I encourage you, while I encourage me, let's look in the mirror today and replace, "Nothing good could come out of me," with Jesus' heart overflowing with love, "I'm crazy about YOU!"

Chapter 13
His Majesty in Missing Pieces

No matter what the missing piece, I am complete in Christ.

Tommy Tyson

With or Without

With the red light flashing in my rear view mirror, it was obvious that the ticket had my name on it. Pulling off the road, I opened my window and strained to hear the officer's words over the thundering beats of my heart.

"You ran the stop sign," he said, peering down at me, "Show me your driver's license."

In that moment I pictured my forgotten purse on the couch at home. Wincing, I answered, "Can I go get my wallet real fast? I live two minutes from here."

Expressionless, he flipped to the right form in the stack of papers atop his icy silver clipboard, "Your name?"

Feeling my sweaty right palm atop my Grandpa's invisible Bible, my goal was honest-to-God accuracy as I answered, "Judith Ann Squier."

"Your address?"

"4113 Alpine Road."

"Your weight?"

I'd answered courteously and clearly, but what to do now? Looking him straight in the eye, I had to say it, "With or without my legs?"

Poker-faced, he didn't flinch. "With your legs."

"Your height?" he continued.

Sitting tall, feeling short, I repeated, "With or without my legs?"

Legs on or legs off has been a daily choice in my world since I received my first set of artificial limbs. Long legs, bending knees, thin ankles, full-size feet, I loved every inch of them. No matter that they were hollow, hewn willow wood, not skin and bones.

No longer dwarf-sized looking up, my legs and I stood eyeball to eyeball with my peers. I joined the "legs" crowd. But quickly I discovered I couldn't keep up with them. Walking was work. I couldn't run, skip, jump rope, jitterbug, water-ski or ascend and descend stairs with ease or speed like my sister. My love affair with my prostheses took a dive.

Immediately the battle of the wills kicked in. A father's love against his daughter's loss of vision. Dad wanted above anything else for his Judy to stand tall or taller in the crowd. Until my dying day, forever etched in my memory is the battle of battles: "You will not go to your confirmation tonight without your legs," my dedicated dad bellowed at me as I crawled down the stairs on my stumps, dressed in my Sunday best, ready to crawl out the door.

Overpowered by his six-foot stature, I pouted but obeyed,

slinking back upstairs, climbing into my "I'm ready when you are" prostheses. Arriving at church too late for the evening program, I was just in time to walk down the aisle to be confirmed.

I walked steadily forward on my earthly father's determination. At sunrise, before he left for work, Dad and I had a standing appointment with my legs. Pulling the stump sock through, first the left socket, then the right, he made sure I was *fully dressed* for the day. Not until I was fifteen did my own determination kick in when I worked as a junior counselor at a camp for the physically disabled. Daily care of children confined to wheelchairs because of cerebral palsy was definitely a *legs on* job. Awakened by the blare of reveille over the cabin's scratchy loudspeaker, I would pull my stump sock through first the left socket, then the right.

My legs and I grew attached to each other. I walked through six years of college, balancing being ambulatory with having a wheelchair handy for maximum speed and mobility. The best step of my life was down the wedding aisle into the arms of my groom. Leaning on my father's strong arm, we both knew a great man awaited me, someone who loved me, with or without my legs!

Ten years into marriage, when we received the good news that I was pregnant, I heard myself say, "That's great, Doctor, but tell me do I deliver my baby with my legs on or my legs off?" Two weeks before my due date, the answer arrived full speed ahead. My legs stood and watched the emergency crew who rushed in to assist me, the woman whose ready-to-be-born baby was crowning. Arriving at Stanford Emergency with just minutes to spare, those same men plus David witnessed what I considered the miracle of miracles: a lady without legs delivering a baby with legs.

"May we stay in the hospital until Emily goes to college," I jokingly asked the discharge nurse, as proud father David loaded mother and daughter into the van to begin a new life of discovery. With trial and error I quickly learned which mothering duties would require legs, and for which ones they could stand off duty, in awe of Baby Squier. For nursing, diaper changing, bathing, we had high stations and low stations so I could be with or without. The logistics fell into place and our baby thrived, thrilling us to the point we agreed, "Let's have more."

The blessings of multiplication were coupled with the

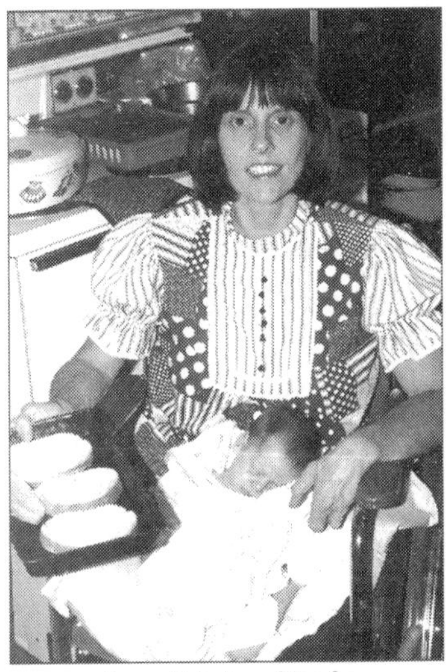

Legs-off Judy and Emily

Legs-on Judy and Emily

amazing discovery of what a set of healthy little legs can do. We rewrote Joni Eareckson Tada's unique song, *May I Borrow Your Hands?* Instead we inserted my missing piece – the legs – so our theme song became, *May I borrow your legs?*

That's the victorious account, but let's face it, I've seen life from down under. Amid all my blessings, if invited, I could instantly broadcast three highlights on my List of Low Points:

- Finding out I was different.
- Facing daily those things I couldn't do.
- Having to wait for and rely on others to do for me what my mind had already done, but my body couldn't.

Even today, I wrestle an opponent who snarls and wants me to believe I'm a loser. I still remember myself, the little crippled girl, like a Pied Piper with an entourage of neighborhood kids staring and mimicking my penguin-like gait through the aisles of our corner grocery store. And like yesterday I remember me, the physically and emotionally exhausted mom, leaving church one Sunday morning. In need of encouragement, I was honest when an acquaintance asked "How's it going, Judy?" Discouraged, I dumped my week of frustration, given two artificial limbs instead of strong legs, for the mountain called mothering three children under five. "You're not a special case. Mothering is impossible PERIOD," barked the lady's heartless reply.

Three things happened that day:

- My self-pity was dealt a death blow.
- I recognized humanity's universal inadequacy

for life's duties.

- My ears percolated to His Majesty's still small voice, lovingly whispering, "Whatever you lack, I am."

"Whatever you lack, I AM." That's it. Life's missing piece. "With" is okay, but "without" is better. Our "lack of" creates a condition of need and our need is a bridge to God. He, and only He, is all-sufficient. Being born without complete legs, I became an artist's studio for God to create a Masterpiece. Simultaneously, as seven times I walked through the rigor of *legmen* manufacturing my artificial limbs, God was invisibly crafting a set of spiritual limbs. Strong. Whole. Eternal. Legs that run to Him. Legs that stand tall in His approval. Legs that depend on His sufficiency alone.

When all is said and done, when Judy-with-no-legs arrives safely Home, my speech is ready, "You done good, Lord. Being born without knees has brought me to my knees. With or without, I stand tall in Thee, my God."

Oh, and the ticket? After all of the questions and all of my answers, the poker-faced cop announced, "I'm not giving you a ticket."

"You aren't giving me a ticket after ALL of this! Why not?"

He responded, still with no expression, "Because you were so honest."

Personally, I think it was because he was still dumbfounded about the legs.

What About You?

What are you living with or without? What have you lost? Maybe bankruptcy has cost you your house, or macular degeneration is stealing your vision, or the inevitable aging process is forcing major life changes.

Don't lose heart. Listen closely to the God of the Universe who is able to meet your every need. "Whatever you lack, I am," He says. The truth is, withouts lose their power when we allow God to fill our missing pieces with Himself. In Matthew 5:4 MSG Jesus says, *You're blessed when you feel you've lost what is most dear to you. Only then can you be embraced by the One most dear to you.*

Can you accept God's embrace and allow Him to prove Himself trustworthy at your point of need? If so, would you join me, all three feet tall of me, and together let's approach His throne and declare our satisfaction with His Majesty's design for us, "With or without, God, we stand tall in Thee."

Chapter 14
His Majesty in Downheartedness

And now to him who can keep you on your feet,
standing tall in his bright presence, fresh and celebrating –
to our one God, our only Savior, through Jesus Christ,
our Master, be glory, majesty, strength, and rule before all time,
and now, and to the end of all time. Yes.

Jude 1:24-25 MSG

Standing Tall

Some days the words, "Thank You, Lord," pop right out of my mouth. Other days they're nowhere to be found. It was on one of those down days that God graciously sent a reminder through my teenage daughter as she downed her Saturday morning breakfast at the kitchen nook.

Seated nearby in my wheelchair at my cutting board desk, I heard myself say, "Emily, you're a teenager, I need your input." I was hoping for the crowning touch for the inspirational speech I would deliver at the Young Life Winter Bash. "What should I be sure and say tonight to a room full of disabled teens and their leaders?"

Awaiting her reply, I realized that this girl had seen me at my best and at my worst. She had become *my legs* as soon as she had learned to walk. She had been with me outside the library the day my artificial limb broke at the ankle and I crashed to the ground. Terrified of mom, I'd wondered if the trauma would scar her for life?

Now more than a decade later I sought Emily's intellectual assist as I had depended on her physical assist. Comfortable with the role of helper, she responded instantly, "Mom, be sure and tell them that you are thankful for your disability."

In all honesty a thankful heart seemed as far removed from me as my legs, standing in the closet at the other end of the house. Still battling the adjustment to a new set of artificial limbs (my sixth set), I felt like a failure. Looking at my soon-to-be woman, I regretted the hikes in the hills, rollerblading, and morning runs we'd never shared. My renegade words startled the Christian Mom I so wanted to model, "Em, I don't think I'm thankful for my disability."

I'd let the cat out of the bag. Would my honesty cancel years of preaching gratitude? I was totally unprepared for my daughter's answer that caused my self-image to stretch until my head almost went through the ceiling.

My daughter validated me in a way that no one else could as she plucked my disability out of the gutter, "Mom, you wouldn't be the woman you are today without it!"

What About You?

What's ambushed you recently? Or throughout your life? Has your store of endurance been exhausted by an unresolved problem? I know the cycle well. A problem knocks you off your feet. When all attempts at solutions fail, self-doubt kicks out self-esteem and "I'm a loser" drowns out "Jesus loves me this I know." You stand as tall as a dandelion during a heat wave.

Strike up the band. The stage is set for Jesus to show up! And when He comes, He brings streams in the desert to your battle weary soul. Maybe He orchestrates His praise through another person or a Bible verse or a hymn that downs your fiery darts of discouragement. He pushes the delete button on all self-hate tapes. He inserts your name in His love song. Triumph eclipses tragedy as He plucks you out of the pit so that now you *stand tall in his bright presence, fresh and celebrating.*

Can you thank God for whatever it is that has bushwhacked you? Even for the lingering shame that has crippled you, stealing your joy and self-worth. May you be humbled but not humiliated, brought to your knees so His Majesty can put you back on your feet, *standing tall in His bright presence, fresh and celebrating.*

Chapter 15
His Majesty in the Everyday

Get down on your knees before the Master;
it's the only way you'll get on your feet.

James 4:10 MSG

Keeping Jesus In

As predictable as Christmas in December was our family's unwelcome letdown a week later. No matter what I did to prevent it the grinch popped up to steal our Christmas joy.

As the girls and I hovered around our kitchen nook finishing off the tail end of the turkey soup, our conversation ricocheted from Emily's *brand new, broken* CD player to Betsy's red Christmas socks. Only God knew how they ended up in a load of white laundry turning everyone's undies, including Papa's, a faded pink. Like the tantalizing presents gone from under the tree, our family's frivolity had soured as the drudgery of cleanup loomed like the ghosts haunting Ebenezer Scrooge.

"How about you girls each carrying five storage containers up to the attic," I bargained, "I'll finish arranging them, then we can have some hot chocolate and the rest of the Christmas cookies." I strained to make myself heard over their unrehearsed, but expected background groans.

As our motley work crew left the kitchen, I spotted two almost forgotten items on the window sill in the family room. Naphy, our youngest and most willing helper, came to my rescue. Trailing behind her sisters, she grabbed the lonely baby Jesus and his lumbering stable and headed upstairs ahead of me. One by one the girls schlepped the bins to their cold storage in the attic.

Exhausted already, I parked my wheelchair at the foot of the stairway, crawled up the steps, and grabbed baby Jesus and the manger waiting by the attic door. Entering, I tucked my head low to avoid the sharp nails that protruded down from the waist high ceiling – evidence that the roof's new shingles were secured in place. My mood matched the chill I felt as I sat on the cold wooden floor boards.

Slowly, the search began for some room in the inn – any old spot would do. I cracked the lid on the bursting-at-the-seams containers nearest to me when suddenly – did I imagine it? Or did I feel a warmth as I cradled baby Jesus in my hand? *Stop everything,* I thought out loud as I awoke from my doldrums. My mind replayed what the family pegged as Mom's post-holiday mantra, "Christmas isn't just one day a year. Christmas is Christ and He is ours to enjoy 365 days a year."

That did it! I tucked Jesus and His manger into my fleece vest, announcing to the spiders and their cobwebs, "I'm keeping you out, Lord."

Judy's year-round nativity

Together He and I wiggled through the knee-high trap door. Down the stairs I barreled – I was on a mission – to return Him to the windowsill next to the couch, my spot to kneel and pray when the girls were at school and their dad was at work.

Keeping Jesus out ultimately translated into *keeping Jesus in.* His Majesty resided in the center of my daily life as a checkpoint and a trigger to trust. I could see Him from the breakfast nook. He watched me as I washed dishes at the kitchen sink. He listened to my phone conversations.

His presence began to influence my behavior. Like the day my minivan and I were challenged by an aggressive truck driver as the road's two lanes narrowed down to one. The other driver won but I crowned myself victor when, stuck behind him, I read his bumper sticker, "How's my driving?" Triumphantly I scribbled down an 800 number which I dialed as soon as I got home. Again on a mission I registered my complaint against the madman behind the wheel. The dispatcher thanked me and informed me that any driver accumulating three complaints would be suspended. Yes!

My sweet vengeance was brief, lasting one night. Kneeling by my windowsill manger the next morning, my conscience squirmed. What was my own rage rating during the previous day's encounter? I, too, was guilty. The 800 number still sat by the phone. The dispatcher I'd talked to the day before answered. I humbly proceeded, "I'm the lady you talked to yesterday. Please cancel my complaint against your driver. I must confess – I, too, was a mad driver."

Did I detect a smile shining from the manger? Seeing the holy Son of God in a humble manger was making a difference in my behavior. The daily reminder provided a moment by moment boost in my ability to surrender my will to life's daily challenges as a mother, a wife, and even as a disabled person. My choice to keep Jesus out all year meant that He and I grew connected at the hip – or the heart. Together we weathered life's highs and inevitable lows. I liked having Him on the scene. That's why when a few years later, Naphy, then an eighth grader sought a topic for an opinion paper in her Government course, I had a ready answer. To her query, "Mom, if you could make one major change in America, what would it be?" I gave this immediate answer, "I would have churches keep Jesus and His manger out year round."

I described for her lines, not traffic lines or grocery store lines, but children and adults one hundred deep waiting for a turn with Jesus and the manger. Twelve months a year, Monday through Sunday, in blizzards, heat waves, and April showers, observing God's humble style, sensing His Presence, learning His ways.

Yes, if keeping Jesus out could change my life, surely He could change others. My gift to America would be to keep Jesus *out* so that He could be *in* the center of our lives.

What About You?

Where is Jesus for you? Is He center stage in your life? Or do you bring Him out of the attic one month a year? Or maybe you've outright told Him, "There's no room in this inn." Actually, He's heard that one before. Not to be deterred, He's been known to wait a lifetime outside of dead-bolted doors.

Have you thought about why He came in the first place? He came because He knew we couldn't do life without Him. He came to make right our wrongs. He came bringing gifts, which include forgiveness, love to us and through us, a purpose for our lives, and energy for the journey. He came to save us.

Oh, how He loves to save our days, every one of them. Like a gentleman, He waits for the door of our hearts to open – a crack is big enough for Him.

Over 2,000 years ago He could be found in a manger. Where might we find Him today? Is today the day you want to welcome the Christ of the manger into your life? He's a simple prayer away, "Jesus, I need You. I invite You to come into my heart to wash me as white as snow. Thank You for coming at Christmas and for dying in my place on the cross. May Your resurrection at Easter become mine. Amen."

If you prayed that prayer, I want to be the first to welcome you into the family of God. You are now a Christian, *Christ In.*

Maybe you accepted Jesus as your Savior years ago at a crusade or with a television evangelist by yourself or even at church. But have you crowned Him Lord? That means acknowledging that everything on earth belongs to Him – beginning with YOU.

May today be your day to place Jesus front and center in your life. If you have a manger set, get it out. Put it in a conspicuous spot as a daily reminder that His Majesty is with you 365 days of every year for the rest of this life. May you make the great discovery that keeping Jesus out translates into keeping Jesus in – in His rightful place at the very center of every detail of your life.

Chapter 16
His Majesty in the Strife

The family, that dear octopus from whose tentacles we never quite escape, nor in our inmost hearts ever quite wish to.

Dodie Smith

God's Masterpiece: The Family

Mornings had become a nightmare. I was ready to turn in my walking papers. Discussions, threats, bribes, mom's prayers – none of these seemed to remove the Monday through Friday day breaking tension. I'd heard that parenting teens would be difficult, but deep down I expected our family would be different, above all that.

Initially I'd felt relief when Emily got her driver's license and could drive herself and Betsy to high school. That was before the horn-honking habit started. Eager to be on time, Betsy would get to the car first and lay on the horn until her sister jumped into the driver's seat. Some mornings the honking would last for minutes.

It was one of those mornings. I half expected the police to drive up and arrest me because my kids were waking the dead. Instead, as the girls' jeep Wrangler sped off to school, I sped my wheelchair to my computer. The following limerick-like poem gushed forth, oozing with maternal frustration and reality, yet crowned with hope:

God's Masterpiece in Process

Papa's hard-of-hearing, Mama's got no legs,
Betsy's got a temper, Emily can hit the dregs.
Naphy's known to tattle, Chester's beat up by Buck.
Joshie whines and shivers.
Herein: the Squier's Muck.
David's got a heart of gold, Judy's got ideas untold.
Emily seeks the peace to make,
Betsy's our family fashion plate.
Naphy's got the gift of helps.
The Squier dogs deliver licks in yelps.
A family is a blend we see, there's bad in you and bad in me.
The gold and good are also there, but not as obvious,
more unaware.
We fight. We yell. It feels like HELL.
We crack. We break. We cry. We ache.
"Behold, My Masterpiece," God proclaims from above,
I'll save your family, I'll teach you to love.
Self-centeredness, rudeness, unkindness, all three
They're tools in My hands to drive you to Me."
So I, a mom, in the midst of this all,
Wholeheartedly pray for God's overhaul.

I confess my contribution to our endless, ugly strife.
Lord, I've taught Your way with my words
But challenged Your will with my life.
Desperate, yet believing I know our God is able,
With His peace, His beauty, this vicious cycle to disable.
And the Squier Family one day will thankfully display
His Redeemed as our label, God's work underway.
The goal to believe I believe I can do.
"To God be All Glory," I'll declare when we're through.
And thanks to the pain, Agape we'll discover
As we behold Christ's image
Miraculously formed in each other.

Funny how early on we all believe our family will be perfect. As parents-to-be we read all the how-to books we can find and off we go. Even with my disability, we had high hopes. It didn't take long to realize there was more missing than Mama's legs. Little by little our family seemed to go berserk, like a bucking bronco out of control.

In desperation, I began a biblical search for the perfect family about the time the girls were in their early teens. I started with the first family in the book of Genesis. Adam and Eve had two sons. One killed the other. Not a great model. Jacob connived to steal both his brother's birthright and blessing. Joseph's ten brothers intended to murder him, but sold him into slavery instead. I imagine sibling pressures were rampant even in Jesus' earthly family since his brothers, James and Jude, refused to believe He was the Son of God until after the

All the Squier Family 1992

The Squier's comic relief photo

resurrection. Where was my model family?

God knows there is no perfect family on earth. That's no surprise to Him. The condemner, on the other hand, clobbers us with, "Look at your family. You should be ashamed!" It took me decades to realize there's no need for shame. My family was "in process" just like every other family on earth. In fact, there was reason to rejoice if the failure in our family could and would drive us to the only perfect parent, our Heavenly Father.

What About You?

What grade do you give your family?

What's missing in your theoretically foolproof plan? Maybe you're a single mom. Maybe you or your spouse struggle with anger. Maybe your teenager is making choices today that you know will ruin him tomorrow. Maybe you're just human beings who aren't very good at loving.

The truth is God is the only hope for any family. He's the only One who can keep that dear octopus from self-destruction. Are you ready to hand yours over to Him? When you do, you can exchange disappointment for the good news that your brokenness sets the perfect stage for God's redemptive work. *And God who started this great work in us will keep at it and bring it to a flourishing finish on the very day Christ Jesus appears.* Philippians 1:6 MSG

So where do you need God to intervene in your family? Ask Him to do it now. He's ready, willing and able, but we have to hand over the broken pieces.

Chapter 17
His Majesty in Turbulence

God, I may fall flat on my face; I may fail until I feel old and beaten and done in. Yet Your love for me is changeless. All the music may go out of my life, my private world may shatter to dust. Even so You will hold me in the palm of Your steady hand. No turn in the affairs of my fractured life can baffle You. Satan with all his braggadocio cannot distract You. Nothing can separate me from Your measureless love.[6]

Ruth Harms Calkin

Saving the Best 'til Last

Grandma's face glowed as her teenage granddaughters harmonized the last *Joy to the World* of Christmas 1994. Her sweet radiance warmed the dank pre-boarding area where our little farewell party hovered outside the security check point in the Bloomington, Illinois airport.

"Mom hasn't looked this joyful since before my Dad died," David whispered.

"She didn't want to miss the fun," his sister Linda remarked apprehensively, obviously unsure of how to handle her aging mom's growing needs.

My mother-in-law's well-being was a definite concern but

our present focus was on getting our family of five back home to California. Small talk and one more hug alternated with listening for the announcement of our plane's arrival. Already late, our departure could be impacted by a threatening snow storm.

My attention ricocheted between our extended farewell, the clock and the dark night outside. My eyes were fixed on the airport's transport chair, ready to carry me with my artificial limbs up the stairway to the St. Louis bound commuter plane, the first leg of our journey home to San Francisco.

Finally we heard the announcement we'd all been waiting for: "Flight 7327 has arrived. Passengers, prepare to board." The words set off a chain reaction. Airport adrenaline kicked in as we hurriedly pitched one guitar, three backpacks, Papa's briefcase, and my cane onto the humming conveyer belt to be x-rayed. Gingerly I leaned forward, gave my purse a toss, quickly spinning my wheelchair backwards.

At that moment, I saw her out of the corner of my eye, smack-dab behind me. My mother-in-law. At 79, trying to move out of my way but slow to react, she began to topple. Like a beloved Christmas tree, slowly, irreversibly our family matriarch went down.

Time stopped. No one moved.

Entering our horror the uniformed security guard spoke calmly, "I work on an ambulance during the day. Don't try to move her."

Stooping down he leaned into Grandma, "Show me where it hurts." Our eyes followed her trembling hand to her left hip.

In one ear we heard, "Which hospital should the ambulance take her to?" In the other ear: "Final boarding call for Flight 7327."

"What are we going to do?" David muttered, looking like he was hoping God would answer. Our shoot-from-the-hip plan was that his sister Linda, who lived in Bloomington, would follow the Grandma-filled ambulance to St. Joseph's Hospital. Our family would fly back to California and call as soon as we got home.

Transferring into the transport chair, wishing I could console my mother-in-law, I was ushered out into the night's chill. The roar of the two engine turbo prop could not drown out the roar from inside me. *Did I break my mother-in-law?*

My thoughts stayed behind in Bloomington as we made our connection in St. Louis then proceeded for a more turbulent than usual flight west to California. My arm muscles replayed wheeling my chair backwards. My eyes replayed seeing my mother-in-law behind me, but I couldn't feel my wheelchair make contact. Did I knock her down or did she trip over her own feet as she tried to move out of my way?

Like a never-ending nightmare, my anxious thoughts tortured me for two thousand miles, flashing back twenty-five years to the day David's mother had written to all the relatives announcing her son's engagement to a *crippled girl*. She and I had never had a conversation about my congenital deformities, my artificial limbs, or my wheelchair. Surprisingly, I'd always felt her respect and acceptance. But did my disability cause her present suffering?

I pondered her decline of late, her slowed mobility with increased imbalance. Drawing from my years as a speech pathologist, I mentally assessed her reduced ability to communicate, her inability to formulate new sentences. I was depressed to think we might never know her version of what happened.

Arriving in San Francisco Airport about midnight, I sensed a dark cloud stalking our drive home.

"Nobody use the phone. I have to check on Grandma." David's words faded as he disappeared through our front door to the phone.

My fear followed him in and watched his every move. "I'm calling about my mom, Violet Squier. Is she a patient there?" David asked the St Joseph Hospital operator. His nod conveyed to me, yes, she was.

His expression was solemn as Linda gave him the update. Then he looked surprised and with his exaggerated whisper, I learned why. "Mom wants to talk to me."

"Hello, Mom," he said eagerly wanting to know she was all right.

I leaned close and strained to hear. *Mmm...* was all she said.

"It's David. How are you, Mom?"

Mmm.

"Mom, we are so sorry about your fall," he tried again.

Mmm.

"Mom, Judy wants me to tell you..."

Suddenly a strong deliberate voice replaced her weak *Mmm*. But strain as hard as I could, I couldn't make out what was said before another *Mmm.*

I squirmed as David poured as much love as humanly possible through the telephone line before hanging up. I winced at the report. X-rays confirmed a broken hip. Surgery was scheduled for the next morning. Mom was on pain medication and very confused. Linda had said she wasn't making any sense at all. I expected the knot in my stomach and the five hundred pound weight of guilt to last forever.

"Oh, there's one more thing," he added. "Mom couldn't talk much but she did manage to say something very clearly when I mentioned your name. She said, "Tell Judy she did not knock me down."

"She said what? How?" I blurted out remembering that his mom wasn't able to form a sentence the whole vacation.

To this day, I can't explain my mother-in-law's ability to utter the sentence that set me free. I simply know that that was the Christmas she saved her best gift 'til last. Not from under the festive adorned tree but from a hospital bed of pain, she gave me a gift I didn't have on my list, one her heart of love knew I needed – peace of mind.

What About You?

What have you agonized over? Where have you found yourself stuck in guilt's torture chamber? Terrible things happen in life. Our inadvertent actions can still harm another and we'd do anything to delete and correct them.

I love Mark Twain's quote: "Forgiveness is the fragrance the violet sheds on the heel that has crushed it." Violet was my mother-in-law's name. How amazing that in her extreme pain, she sensed my extreme need and cleared my record.

Come to think of it, that's what Jesus came to do – right our wrongs and replace condemnation with love. Like Violet, God sensed our extreme need, and while in extreme pain, cleared our record. *Think of it! All sins forgiven, the slate wiped clean, that old arrest warrant canceled and nailed to Christ's Cross.* Colossians 2:14 MSG

His forgiveness is universal, but each of us must make it personal. John 3:16 NASB my first Bible memory verse as a child, sums it up: *For God so loved the world that He gave His only begotten Son, that whoever believes in Him should not perish, but have eternal life.*

God has a clean slate with your name on it. Corrie ten Boom liked to say, "He throws our sins into the deepest sea and puts up a *No Fishing* sign."

Peace of mind cost God dearly. It is ours when we are His. His Majesty, the Prince of Peace, can set you free. He's the only One who can.

Chapter 18
His Majesty in Cold Feet

Courage is fear that has said its prayers.

Author Unknown

Courage Begins with Fear

"I'll be so embarrassed if they recognize me," I thought when I noticed the two firemen in the local grocery store's checkout line ahead of me.

My mind flashed back to the day I'd never forget – the day four firemen barreled into our back bedroom where I lay traumatized by childbirth – my contractions five minutes apart. Those men had gotten an eyeful. Not only had they seen a woman fully exposed in childbirth but their *woman in distress* was a double amputee with a set of artificial limbs standing beside the bed.

That day's excruciating birth pains were compounded by the fact I couldn't fathom how I could deliver a baby when I lacked legs to push. I cringe to think legs weren't the only thing missing that day. My hysterical shouts, "Help me, help me, please help me!" proved I had not one ounce of courage.

For the next fifteen years I'd prayed, "Lord, may I never

cross paths with the men who witnessed the lowest point of my life."

But what if these two guys had been there? Curiosity booted modesty out the door as I spoke softly to the uniformed men in front of me, "By any chance, did either of you ever show up to deliver a baby in the house a mile down the road?"

The fireman closest to me acknowledged that indeed he had been there and yes, he remembered me. But what he would never forget was that I was so brave! That was all he said, before he picked up his bag of groceries and exited the store.

I stood there, dumbfounded. Brave? Me? How could that be? That's not the first time Much Afraid Me was dubbed a Brave Heart. More than once someone has glanced from my smile down to the place in my wheelchair where legs are supposed to be and said, "Surely, you could teach this world about courage."

Actually, the truth is, my cold feet could teach the world about fear. Fear that met me on operating tables, but was never talked about at the dinner table because we were all play-acting courage. Fear that sat next to me when no one else would. Fear that taunted, "You're super glued to the sidelines. Don't expect a life."

Funny how Christians, in particular, seem afraid to admit fear. Are they afraid that fear isn't godly? What about run-and-hide Moses and Gideon, and the disciples who scattered when Jesus was arrested, put on trial, beaten and then crucified?

For me courage is fear that is brave enough to admit, "God, I can't do this," to which He replies "You're so right, my child. Allow Me!" That's when my quaking heart wells up with newfound courage. Courage without end because it's His courage.

What About You?

What has been your most embarrassing moment? The lowest point in your life? Perhaps you or someone you love has received a jail sentence. Or your family has recently declared bankruptcy. Or it's you who is attending Overeaters Anonymous.

When I am going down for the count, Annie Johnson Flint's words from her hymn, *He Giveth More Grace,* come to my rescue like a life preserver to a gasping swimmer:

When we have exhausted
our store of endurance,
when our strength has failed
ere the day is half done,
when we reach the end
of our hoarded resources,
our Father's full giving has only begun.[7]

What do we do when our knees are knocking and our strength fails? Could it be that our horrifying lowest point is God's designated holy ground? Our seeming catastrophe can become a blessing in disguise when our last breath gasps, *For this I have Jesus!* The minute we welcome Jesus on the scene, His Majesty transcends our lowest point so that we Much Afraids are seen as pillars of strength, not because we have courage, but because we have Him.

CHAPTER 19

His Majesty in Discouragement

Most of us, swimming against the tides of trouble
the world knows nothing about,
need only a bit of praise or encouragement
and we will make the goal.

Jerome P. Fleishman

POOLSIDE COMFORT

It was my birthday. The phone rang just as I was ready to leave for my morning swim. "Happy Birthday to the birthday girl," said my mother as my sister Tina chimed in.

After a brief conversation, my well wishers sent their hugs and ended the chat with the story of a recent event they said reminded them of me. They'd been at a restaurant when a young couple arrived with a newborn baby. Everyone *oohed* and *aahed* over what was inside the pink blanket. For some unexplained reason, Tina finished by saying, "Judy, Mom reminisced about your birth when there were no *oohs* and *aahs.*"

Some happy birthday! With a heavy heart, I hung up the phone, went out and pulled my wheelchair into the car, crawled into the driver's seat and drove next door to the swim club. My spirit continued to sink as I lowered my wheelchair into the parking lot and pondered the pain my birth defect and I had brought upon my family.

As I wheeled through the gate at the club, I was greeted by my friend Kate, a master swimmer who does 2000 meters per work out compared to my 750. Sensing my pain, she squatted down to eye level, drawing as near to my wheelchair as she could. Few people think to do that. When they do, my self-worth stands six feet tall. Caring Kate was just what His Majesty knew I needed. We didn't say much but Kate's warm demeanor hugged every cell of my being.

After we said our good byes, I found an empty lane, jumped into the water, and began my workout. I, the legless birthday girl, sporting my goggles, nose clip, and snorkel, prayed for a birthday blessing. As was my custom, I meditated on a Bible passage as I swam:

I saw God before me for all time.
Nothing can shake me; he's right by my side.
I'm glad from the inside out, ecstatic;
I've pitched my tent in the land of hope.
I know you'll never dump me in Hades;
I'll never even smell the stench of death.
You've got my feet on the life-path
with your face shining sun-joy all around.

Acts 2:25-28 MSG

With each lap came a splash of possibility. "Yes, Lord, You are right by my side, swimming in that lane next to me. I am not alone. Please show me Your face today," I pleaded. Back and forth across the pool I went, all 30 lengths. My goggled eyes looked for His face *shining sun-joy all around.* But the only face I saw was Kate's, freckled, smiling, loving me. "Wait a minute," I argued, "Kate isn't a believer. Is it possible to see Your face in the face of an unbeliever, Lord?"

From prior conversations, I knew that Kate did not believe Jesus was the Son of God nor did she want to receive Him as her Savior and Lord. Yet I felt God's Spirit telling me Kate's face was His Face *shining sun-joy all around.* Finally my hungry heart sidestepped my confused mind allowing His joy to wash over me through her joy. Immediately I became *glad from the inside out – ecstatic.*

I hurried through my shower so that I could get home and call Kate. She didn't answer so I left a message, "Kate, thank you for being there for me today. I want you to know that I saw God's face *shining sun-joy* through you to me."

Kate didn't call me back. Not until a few weeks later did we bump into one another in the dressing room at the club. From one shower stall to the other, with timidity mixed with boldness, I asked her if she'd received my phone message. Yes, she had, and with a mix of humility and sincerity she answered, "Your message was an honor, Judy. I always thought of God out there somewhere. Your words brought Him inside."

What About You?

We all carry wounds from our childhood – no matter how hard our parents tried to protect us. Some have been abused by a neighbor or even a family member. Or teased unrelentingly in school. Maybe you were the last to be chosen for a relay race. Who of us doesn't need and welcome encouragement, some days more than others?

God is omniscient and knows our needs and He's the controller of all things. Put those two together and you have permission to expect His Majesty to show up when you're down. The Israelites marked His appearances with memorial stones. I call them "God sightings," meaning He does something to demonstrate His Love for me.

I smile when I remember the things, especially the little things, God has done to cheer me on. An unexpected call from a friend is nice. But more than that, God knows my love language and often wraps His love in things I love. This Christmas Eve day I had a visitor – a black bird with no feet – who perched in a planter right beside me in my wheelchair. I love birds and I have a kinship with those with disabilities. God's gift of that feathered friend was my holiday highlight.

What has His Majesty orchestrated to individualize His love for you? Who has He used to throw you the life preserver when you were bobbing up for your last breath? May I suggest you send that someone a thank you? In God's perfect timing, it may be just the encouragement they need to get through today.

CHAPTER 20
His Majesty in the Unforseen

There are only two ways to live your life:
one as though nothing is a miracle;
the other as though everything is a miracle.
Albert Einstein

WEDDING MIRACLES

I never expected to get married. I figured growing up with a disability excluded me from most of life's givens. My inner voice shot down any glimmer of hope: *Why would a guy settle for damaged goods when he could choose from countless women with whole bodies?*

Going away to college opened up the world for me. Participating in the University of Illinois' Rehabilitation Department with 200 other disabled students meant that I was integrated into a campus experience with 20,000 able-bodied students. Tim Nugent, the program's founder, leveled the playing field for us by eliminating architectural barriers. In addition to a college education, we all gained a new lease on life. He proved to us that a disability need not disqualify us from life's options.

I left the university with a Master's Degree in Speech Pathology and accepted a job offer about the same time I said *yes* to a marriage proposal from David Squier. I was amazed to see how my disability was a nonissue for him. Watching me hoist myself into his convertible sports car didn't phase him, nor did he seem bothered about putting my shoe back on my artificial foot on our first date. Never did he mind that his wife's artificial limbs stood beside the bed at night.

Together we learned what activities in life were *legs on* jobs and which ones were *legs off*. Over time I added a third category, *That's a legs job. I don't go there!* The Bible warns us that, *We can make our plans but the final outcome is in God's hands. We can always "prove" that we are right, but is the Lord convinced?* Proverbs 16:1-2 TLB

God had changed the plan when He walked me head-on into my *I'll never be a mother*. With three growing daughters, the stage was being set for me to walk head-on into another *I don't go there*. The day was growing ever closer for me to be the mother-of-a-bride. *But that's a legs job!* I thought to myself the day our daughter Emily announced her engagement and wrote the word *wedding* on our calendar. Panic gripped me as I visualized endless treks through miles of stores, photography studios, florists, caterers and bakeries. Fear pinned me to the mat as I anticipated the moment in the wedding when the bride and groom's moms ascended the steps to the altar to light the wedding candles.

As expected, Emily's wedding knocked me off my feet. The normal wedding preparations were complicated by my own personal issues. Were the church and reception sites fully accessible? Would I walk down the aisle or ride in my wheelchair? My sixth set of artificial limbs balked at the possibility. I could barely stand in my own kitchen.

And yet, in the final analysis, life happens. The fast track called a WEDDING – with its hundreds of hours of planning, shopping, decision making, plus the expenditures of not just money but time and energy – comes and goes. Then we kick back, savor the memory and assess the process.

I was right. The mother-of-the-bride assignments provided enough leg work to exhaust an octopus. Not everywhere we went was wheelchair accessible. Several times my bride-to-be daughter had to pull my wheelchair and me up steps. She never complained.

Weddings are a sure cure for self-sufficient souls who refuse help. My friends rallied around me. They showed up as personal shoppers, shower hostesses, wedding coordinators and hors d'oeuvre caterers. "Your wish is my command." Friend Nita pulled me aside and said her wedding gift would be to help *me* find shoes. Daughter Betsy (who by now preferred Elizabeth) marched me from store to store until we landed the perfect gold dress. "Mom, you look gorgeous," she exclaimed, building in me a confidence I didn't have.

On the wedding day, another girlfriend dressed in a tuxedo, chauffeured the newlyweds in her husband's red and white '57 Chevy convertible. My sister Tina, functioned as my Siamese twin and let me borrow her legs. And I, a do-it-myself diehard, learned to accept help.

In the end, the wedding taught me to trust my kids' sensitivity to my special needs. Without prior discussion my daughter altered the candle-lighting ceremony, so that the dads brought the candles down the steps to the moms. "That was a good idea to involve the fathers," one of our friends commented, "I hope our kids do the same thing."

And in all the excitement, I'm thankful to say I didn't miss the small wonders. The floral designer made sure I knew that the yellow roses selected for the bride's bouquet were *Judy roses*. Funny how God could use a flower to tell me that I was handpicked by Him to mother this child. Banished forever were my unspoken fears that she had suffered because of my disability.

Emily's Wedding Day

And surprise of surprises, two weeks later while viewing the wedding video, daughter Elizabeth commented excitedly, "Mom, you *walked* down the aisle."

"You're right, Elizabeth, I did!" I, too, was surprised having see-sawed for weeks between should I walk or should I ride? Seemingly on auto-pilot my new bronze-colored flats, tracked down by Nita, walked sure footedly down the church's white wedding carpet.

And when all was said and done, the bubbles blown, and the guests gone, the joyous bride plopped down on my lap for a mommy hug. With her gown cascading down the front of my wheelchair, this mother-daughter photo is my number one pick of the 450 taken by the San Francisco photographer. It's the photo that shouts: MIRACLES HAPPEN.

Thirty five years earlier I had been the bride that I never expected to be. I mothered children I never expected to bear. And together my daughter-bride and I embraced one another on the miracle day in both of our lives.

What About You?

What miracle have you witnessed in your life? Maybe you never expected to graduate from high school, much less college. Maybe you never expected to survive a stage IV breast cancer diagnosis. Or possibly you or your child have been set free from a lifetime of bondage to drugs, alcohol or food? Applaud the Miracle Worker who knew your heart's desire and granted it. Take time to savor the wonder of the new you that seemed miles beyond your reach.

And remember God's miracles don't end with us. They extend to the next generation and the next so that together – moms and dads, children and grandchildren – arm in arm can stand in awe of His Majesty's masterpieces.

Years ago, the girls and I loved to sing Ruth Harms Caulkin's kid's chorus: *My God is so big so strong and so mighty. There's nothing my God cannot do.*[8]

Is your God so big? If so, let's shout it from the rooftops, *There's nothing my God cannot do!*

Chapter 21
His Majesty in Affliction

But He knows the way I take,
when He has tried me,
I shall come forth as gold.

Job 23:10 NASB

My Gold Shoe

I'd always wished I'd kept my deformed feet when they were amputated. My sentimental side would have welcomed a foot-filled jar on the shelf in the hall closet next to the Mason jar containing the rattlesnake that David killed. To this day, I try to remember which foot had two toes and which one had three. Either way the grand total was five.

Those feet never did fit into ordinary shoes so I wore high-top orthopedic shoes until I was ten. Artificial limbs opened a new world for me with their standard-size feet. Hey, how many people get to choose their foot size? That was a no brainer, "I'll take a six and a half narrow, like my sister's."

One of my first outings after receiving my prostheses was a trip to the local shoe store. In marched our family of four with Dad announcing, "Pick out anything you want, Judy." A few hours later we exited with a pile of shoe boxes up to the sky. Black patent leather, tan, white, olive green, red, navy blue shoes and my dream come true – a pair of burgundy penny-loafers. This rite of passage canceled my previously limited selection of boring brown or washed-out-white orthopedic shoes, which the brace man would rivet to a set of metal stilts.

Families coping with disability often see caregiving as a lifetime commitment. Mom and Dad were as surprised as I was when I left home for good. They reacted like mice released from a cage, scurrying from continent to continent, becoming world travelers. Mom's first love was shopping. Her collections burst the seams of our small brick house west of Chicago. We'd laughingly say George Carlin's quote, *Home is where you keep your stuff while you go out and buy other stuff,* was written for our mother. Meanwhile Dad loved restoring discards of any type – everything that came out of his hobby shop was a treasure.

One day Dad was rummaging through some rubble in the garage when he unearthed a treasure that triggered an avalanche of emotion. "Judy's stilts." His words referenced the biggest challenge of his life and seeing them unleashed decades of memories of life's heartaches and hurdles. Rubbing his hand across the icy cold metal, he instantly knew what he would do.

Returning to the house, he descended the steep staircase to the cellar, through the musty basement he went to his hobby shop. Surrounded by his well-used tools, he placed one of the stilts in a vice and carefully removed a well-worn shoe. Gently he dusted it off, selected a can of gold spray paint and pressed the nozzle. Pleased with the finished product, he hurried upstairs and presented it to my mom– a gold shoe. That shoe sat in a place of prominence in their home until their next visit to California when he proudly presented it to me, the mother of three little girls whose shoe collections included every color of the rainbow.

Seeing the now-gold shoe reminded me of the stark contrast between my early years and those of my daughters, with their lineup of flip flops, soccer shoes, ballet shoes, Sunday shoes and everyday shoes. Holding it triggered an avalanche of memories – the years of exclusion and isolation, disappointment and frustration that were no more. I'd survived and had come out the other end, standing – not just standing but standing tall. The fact is Dad didn't paint the shoe during our wilderness years. He couldn't. But after I'd graduated from college, married, enjoyed a fulfilling career and was now a mom, he couldn't not paint it.

Immediately the tried-by-fire treasure was given a place of prominence in our home. I smile now when I remember that our girls were instructed, "In case of fire, grab Mom's legs and Mom's gold shoe." That shoe had been refined in God's fire pit and so had we. All of us, each one of us had scuff marks that God Himself had made shine – frustrations that birthed creativity, pain that bred compassion, loss that became gain.

My shoe accompanies me when I give speeches about His Majesty in Brokenness. It's traveled with me all over the

Judy's gold shoe

world. It's been cradled and even kissed by individuals and family members beaten down by disability. Ironically, the shoe, which wouldn't bring a nickel in a thrift store, has become a symbol of hope. My shoe and I provide living proof:

- God makes no mistakes.
- Jesus redeems all of life's pain.
- His Majesty shines blindingly bright in human brokenness.

As I finish my talks, I reach deep into my prized shoe and retrieve a gold paper, wrinkled and worn, containing a Bible verse that explains for me why human suffering is worth it!

My troubles turned out all for the best. They forced me to learn from your textbook. Truth from your mouth means more to me than striking it rich in a gold mine.

Psalm 119:71 MSG

What About You?

What is your trophy hewn out of brokenness? What symbolizes your God-made treasure crafted from your once-detested suffering?

My friend Annie's trophy is the little bell her ailing mom rang in the middle of the night. Awakening Annie from a deep sleep, the bell signaled her to come quickly, mom needs you. Now that her mom is safely Home, Annie prizes the very object that once was burdensome.

Dale Evans Rogers' book *Angel Unaware* offers a loving tribute to her trophy – her baby, Robin, born with a diagnosis of mongolism, now called Down syndrome. My friend George, a brother in Christ, would have named his terminal brain tumor as his trophy, his sooner-than-expected ticket to glory.

What is making you bleed right now? What is the last thing in this world you could imagine becoming your trophy? Actually that object – be it a shoe, a bell, a much-loved human being or even a terminal disease – is only an earthly symbol of the real prize – our golden faith, which when tested and purified, is more precious to God than mere gold.

I add my *Alleluia* to the Apostle Peter's exhortation to keep the faith:

So be truly glad! There is wonderful joy ahead, even though the going is rough for a while down here. These trials are only to test your faith, to see whether or not it is strong and pure. It is being tested as fire tests gold and purifies it and your faith is far more precious to God than mere gold...

I Peter 1:6-7a TLB

Chapter 22

His Majesty in Exposed Shame

...Who heals all your diseases;
Who redeems your life from the pit;
Who crowns you with loving kindness and compassion...

Psalm 103:3b-4 NASB

Stump Washing

I've never been able to hide my brokenness, but I've taken great care to hide my shame. My swim suits have always sported a skirt to protect my *residual limbs* from curiosity seekers. My Bermuda shorts have been long enough to cover what's inside.

But one day, I was caught off guard at a Joni and Friends Family Retreat Leadership Training. The day had been filled with instruction about disabilities, hands-on activities with wheelchairs, and Biblical teaching about God's perspective on brokenness. The trainees were a mix of teenagers and adults – short term missionaries – who would be assigned to a family with a disabled member. These brave volunteers had varying degrees of exposure to disabilities – some had a disabled family member, while others had never seen a broken toe.

For me the day had been a piece of cake. With half a century of life with a disability under my belt, I knew all the answers. My mind was wandering. "No challenges here," I thought.

It was all good until the retreat director announced, "We're going to end our training time together with A FOOT WASHING ceremony." His words booted my confidence off its perch as fear and shame kicked in. Avoiding eye contact I surveyed the room. Were there any other amputees? No, everyone in the room had feet to wash, except me.

I listened as the facilitator continued, "Jesus, the King of Kings knelt down and washed His disciples' stinky feet." My mind heard *stinky stumps*. I watched as a large Tupperware bowl with some towels was placed in the center of our circle. My attention ricocheted from the bowl to the door as I planned my escape route. My defenses bared their teeth, "No way will I do this. Bare my shame? Never!"

Feeling the wind of relief in my hair, I wheeled myself out the door and down the ramp, muttering a triumphant, "I'm out of here!"

It was a year or so later. I was facilitating the first planning meeting for an upcoming women's retreat. Half a dozen of us in leadership gathered to brainstorm the options in our desire to do something different. With our creative juices flowing and our list of ideas growing, I threw out my No-No. "Just so you all know, if you plan to have a foot washing ceremony, I'm out of there."

The weekend of the retreat arrived. Workshop leaders, the prayer coordinator, musicians, the keynote speaker – we all gathered a few hours ahead of time to set up. I watched in fascination as Shelley unpacked her goodies for her Daughters of the King: God's Princesses workshop. Out popped a sparkling crown, a glitzy treasure box, and a jar filled with fluorescent gems. Almost done, she looked at me with a proud smile and announced, "I brought this just in case." Her hands lovingly cradled an heirloom – her grandma's crystal bowl – containing two spankin' new yellow wash rags.

"Just in case, what?" I asked.

"Just in case you okay a stump washing!" she said with an air of optimism.

"No way, Shelley!" I said, my words marking my boundary in cement.

The three-day retreat moved quickly as they always do. On the last morning, the leaders met privately together to pray, energized with stories of God touching lives. Suddenly Marti, our music leader, announced, "We need to pray for Judy and her upcoming mission trip to Romania."

Yes! I was eager to be prayed over since the thought of traveling to a third world country in a wheelchair terrified me. I propelled my wheelchair to center stage, threw up my hands and shouted, "Pray for me!"

A dozen women gathered round. Their heartfelt concern plucked me from life's sidelines. As their prayers welled up, my defenses fell down. The touch of their hands poured God's healing love into my wounds. My self-consciousness evaporated so that suddenly I had nothing to hide.

Opening my eyes just a crack, I saw Shelley kneeling

down in front of me. A voice from somewhere deep inside of me barked, "Get the bowl!"

"Get the bowl?" Unbelief filled her response.

"Get the bowl."

She'd given up hope and had already packed the bowl away in her car, but she hurried out to retrieve it. Prayers continued to flow as Shelley returned. Not wanting to chill me, she poured hot water from an insulated decanter into the bowl, intending to cool it with tap water. Unfortunately, she wasn't fast enough. A few gasps joined the prayers as Grandma's beautiful crystal bowl gave a loud crack, spilling the hot contents onto Shelley's arm. Not to be deterred, Shelley-on-a-mission grabbed a pitcher filled with lukewarm water and returned to the huddle placing the ceremonial utensils in front of my wheel chair.

Intercepted by love, my lifelong shame felt like a debutante as stumps peeked out of my skirt. Two close friends, Mary and Annie, now kneeling in front of me, ever so gently washed my brokenness. One washed the right; the other washed the left. By now the roomful of prayers had turned into sobs and then sobs turned into wailing. It sounded like the Wailing Wall in Old Jerusalem. Interesting that I shed not one tear. Why would I? For me it was a time to rejoice. The roomful of wailers were validating my life's bucket of silent tears. Engulfed in love, the shaming part of me was silenced and the long-imprisoned Judy was set free.

"What an amazing experience!" We couldn't stop talking about it as Mary, Nita and I drove home over the mountain.

"What happened?" I asked. "Why was everyone so emotional?" We talked around it for a long time, until finally we got it: When a person goes public with their shame, deep healing happens both inside and around them. My coming out of hiding brought us all out of hiding. My public display of brokenness allowed others to release their deadbolts. Set free from self-centeredness and condemnation, together we beheld His Majesty kneeling down, washing our stinky feet and stumps. Our Wounded Healer, who bore not only our sins but also our shame on the cross, shattered the carefully guarded brokenness of a roomful of women just as the hot water had shattered Grandma's heirloom bowl.

We were almost home after our mountain top experience in California's Santa Cruz Mountains. We'd talked ourselves out and were quietly savoring what God had just done, when suddenly my bosom buddy, Nita, announced from the back seat, "I have one complaint about the retreat. I wanted to wash a stump, Judy!"

What About You?

What is the source of your life's shame? What do you strategically try to hide from the world? Are you afraid to speak because you stutter? Did you have an abortion and regret it? Were you fired from your job? Do you have a criminal record? Were you abused as a child or molested as an adult? What do you have deadbolted shut?

Jesus is kneeling outside the door today, longing to embrace you and wash away the shame associated with your brokenness. Shame that has imprisoned you. Shame that blocks your ability to receive the love of God and others. Jesus came to pluck each one of us out of the pit. His wounds, represented by His crown of thorns, canceled the curse. He brought instead a crown of love and compassion with your name on it. When we understand that, the healing process can begin. Yes, it is a process. Decades of accumulated condemnation don't vanish overnight. The grave clothes come off layer by layer. Yes, they do come off.

Remember the prayers prayed for my trip to Romania? My expectation as a team member with Becky's Hope was to help Romanian moms with disabled children in their healing process in a country where disability is even more shameful than here. But God had a much greater plan that included not only healing their shame, but more of mine.

Healing happens when we are willing to let Jesus wash away

the dirt from our lives. Are you willing to allow that? Kneeling in front of us, we can't miss the crown of thorns on His head. After washing away our shame, He reminds us that He wore the crown of condemnation in our place. His sacrificial love bought His Beloveds – that's you and me – crowns of beauty, loving kindness, and compassion. Are you wearing your crown?

Chapter 23

His Majesty When the Silence is Broken

Though the world is full of suffering,
it is also full of the overcoming of it.

Helen Keller

Giving Voice to the Pain

"Lord, You must be kidding!" Despite the plane tickets on my kitchen counter and an imminent departure date on my calendar, I still couldn't believe God would call me to an international ministry. *That's a legs job, God!*

In fear and trembling, remembering Jonah and not wanting to take up residence in the belly of a whale, I had agreed to go relying on His Majesty every step of the way.

In preparation, I sought the counsel of our pastor Brian Morgan, who guided me with, "Judy, your mission trip to Romania is an opportunity to tell your story. Before you go write your story and your poem, not tales of triumph but of brokenness. Your authenticity will provide an international stage on which your audience can embrace their own pain. Then together you can see God fling open the gateway to heaven."

Guided by God's Spirit I wrote the whole truth and nothing but the truth.

I took off my mask and told it like it was. As I shared my story with audiences in Eastern Europe and later in America, we repeatedly saw heaven's gate open as our pain came eyeball to eyeball with His Majesty, who had pitched His tent in the midst of our brokenness.

As I met with the parents of disabled children in Romania, I shared:

My Story

Mom says she thanked God for my perfectly formed head and for my big brown eyes. What she didn't say was that my birth brought her excruciating pain and that her heart broke as the world came to gawk at her broken baby.

A huge elephant named PAIN accompanied us home from the hospital, invading Reverend and Mrs. Rieder's parsonage in upstate New York – draining, isolating, DISABLING. But the Rieders came from strong stock and conjured up the strength to survive. "How are you?" brought mechanical "Fine, thank you's," camouflaging the buzzard named Hopelessness.

Mechanically hymns were sung and the Good Book was read. Dad became purpose driven – on a mission to seize the best life possible for his little girl without complete legs. Mom stayed stuck in the pain, acquiring a disability on the inside that exceeded my disability on the outside.

Pain? Interesting how no one talked about the pain. Words might make it worse. We believed that lie.

Mom performed the dailies and shopped in between. My sister Tina was worth her weight in gold as I lived my eventless childhood and teen years vicariously through her full calendar.

Miraculously, my life began in college. Love met me through David Squier, followed by marriage, a career, motherhood – three children. I'd arrived! But a sense of failure greeted and depleted me at every accomplishment. A victorious, inspiring woman of God on the outside, the lie of I'm no good caused me to cower on the inside. Self-hate shackled my spirit and canceled my self-worth.

But not forever. In 2004 the lights went on. Thanks to a Christian counselor, my mute emotions finally received permission to articulate how it really felt: "Disability stole my childhood. It usurped my essence."

Speaking the truth can set us free. Articulating pain breaks down strongholds of shame: "Honest to God? I'm not to blame for Mom's pain?"

Discarding the mirage of strength and cheerfulness, I shout to Jesus: "Save me, Lord!"

Up from the basement to Jesus' lap, I bask in the truth, "I am lovable."

At last my wholeness catches up with my Holiness and I stand tall: A Daughter of the King.

My Poem

Broken.
Cursed at birth.
Loved.
Applauded.
Yet pained, blamed, chained.
Afraid to complain.
Daybreak, Sonrise.
Set free.
Permission to be me.
Honesty.
"I hate my disability.
I hate the thief who robbed me of legs
and barred me from the world of legs.
I'm sad. I'm mad.
At the same time, I'm glad."
GOD SAVED THE DAY.
Amazingly His light shines blindingly bright through
Broken People
LIKE ME.
Judith Ann Rieder
Judy
Mrs. David Squier
God's Sanctified Escort
to lead others from
the pit
to PRAISE.

What About You?

What shame and pain have you kept muzzled that needs a voice? What stretch the truth tale of triumph could use a reality check? It's time to tell the truth, the whole truth and nothing but the truth, so help you God. Yes, He will help. *The Lord is near to the brokenhearted and saves those who are crushed in spirit.* Psalm 34:18 NASB

Exposing our shame renders it powerless. That's the beauty of drug and alcohol addiction support groups, which have now expanded into support groups to address overeating, overspending, depression, phobias, codependency, sex/pornography problems and more. But we all look so healthy!

The truth is we're all broken in some way, be it physically, mentally, emotionally, intellectually, socially or spiritually. Humanity shares a common diagnosis: broken people in need of a mender. Do you know the Mender? He has pitched His tent in the midst of your brokenness and is eager to bring healing and wholeness.

Are you ready to come out of hiding? Writing your story and poem would be a good place to start. Then ask Him who He knows needs to hear them. Wrapped in His love, read them so that together you can see God fling open the gateway to heaven.

Chapter 24
His Majesty in the Long-Overdue Dialogue

For out of His fullness
we all received one grace after another
and spiritual blessing upon spiritual blessing,
and even favor upon favor and gift heaped upon gift.

John 1:16 AMP

The Gift

I noticed her right away. Eighteen-year-old Noletta atop her adult-sized three-wheeled bike at the retreat center in Brasov, Romania. Her mother had misunderstood. Not realizing the retreat was for moms only, she had brought her teenage daughters, Noletta and her younger sister.

My sister Tina and I, still a bit jet-lagged, had come to Eastern Europe with two other Americans at the invitation of Lidia Oprean, founder of Becky's Hope. Lidia's daughter Becky, born with spina-bifida sixteen years earlier, had taught her mom life-changing lessons about God's presence in suffering – lessons which Lidia wanted to share with other moms of disabled children. We prayed these eighty women who had come from all over Romania would come to know our God, who had pitched His tent in our pain, walked with us, and carried us when necessary. “Lord, perform Your healing work,” we whispered that first morning as we assembled in the worship center at the former KGB headquarters.

Noletta drew my attention as she smiled shyly but didn’t speak when I greeted her. *No dialogue with her*, I thought, as her expressive brown eyes darted quickly toward her sister who spoke for both of them. The mother and daughters spent the morning seated together in back of the back row against the far wall.

I noticed the threesome again after lunch. Noletta was sitting silently behind her mother and sister, watching them enjoy the craft we’d brought from America – decorating large wire butterflies with multi-colored beads. I saw her again in the evening, left alone on her bed as her mother and sister joined our group at the dormitory stairwell for a spontaneous hymn sing. Lonely Noletta reminded me of once-lonely Judy.

Silent Noletta, always an observer never a participant, I thought to myself the next day as I saw her expressionless face watching a dozen happy moms making beautiful greeting cards.

“Do you want to make one?” I asked as I maneuvered my wheelchair beside her.

“I can’t,” she replied, glancing at her hands in her lap.

“I didn’t know you could talk,” I blurted out shocked to find out not only did she speak clearly, but she spoke in fluent English. All week I had waited while interpreters translated my speeches.

"She learned English watching television," her sister spoke up.

Watching television. This girl's brilliant!

Deciding silent Noletta had untapped potential, I picked up a greeting card from the table in front of us – the card with a vibrant red rose that her sister had artistically decorated and I asked, "Would you like to write a letter to your mother?"

She smiled an enthusiastic yes, but declined the green felt pen I offered. So I played secretary. "What do you want the letter to say?" I asked.

A shrug of her shoulders communicated she didn't know.

"Do you want me to tell you what I would write to my mother?" I asked, knowing that our mothers had both given birth to a disabled child.

Her big smile provided a clear yes, so I began to dictate. She nodded approval for each line before I wrote it:

> *My Dear Mom,*
> *I am sorry for all the pain my disability has*
> *brought you. I love you very much.*
> *When we get to heaven, I will wait on you*
> *hand and foot.*

"Is it okay?" I asked.

She was pleased with the letter and surprised me by taking the green pen to sign her name. Her penmanship was perfect.

"Shhhhh, don't tell your mom," I whispered as she agreed to my proposal that she read the letter in front of the whole group during the final time of sharing. Her enthusiasm knit our hearts together as we anticipated this special gift for her mother.

Entering the worship center the next day, I was alarmed to discover Noletta's reserved spot in the back of the back of the room empty. Did she get cold feet? Not at all. She was sitting on her bike in my spot in the front row eager to read her letter and more. When Grace, one of our song leaders, had overheard our conversation the day before and realized Noletta could speak, she invited her to join in a duet and even invited her to choose the song.

We were both surprised when silent Noletta selected a song she'd only heard once before – a song Grace had written based on Psalm 139's teaching about God's loving presence in utero carefully creating each one of us. Grace was astonished at her choice, "That song is five minutes long! Are you sure you want to sing that one?"

Noletta was sure. As eighty people settled into the room, Noletta headed to the stage, maneuvering her bike back and forth several times until she was in the middle aisle between the rows of chairs. Grace stood beside her, holding the microphone close to her mouth. Showing only a wee bit of apprehension, Noletta sang like a pro, giving the impression she had rehearsed for weeks, not just minutes.

When the applause quieted, she stayed put – center stage. Holding high the brightly colored rose card, she read with clarity and sincerity. Her Romanian words flowed over the heads of the spellbound women to her mother seated in the

Romania 2004 Judy, Noletta and her Mom

back. From silent Noletta came the heart's cry of every disabled person:

I'm sorry.
Thank you.
Someday I'll make
it up to you.

No one moved as Noletta's mom stood and walked down the aisle to the front of the room. Healing words flowed straight from her heart, forming a bridge across the great chasm of isolation to her daughter, "You have never been a burden to me. You are a gift from God."

As she continued to talk, my ears heard her words in my own mom's voice. The dialogue of healing I'd longed for my entire life was happening in Romania. I, the disabled one born with severe deformities, remembered the decades of my own mother's pain. Her shame when the church implied her sin caused my disability. Her fears each time I went to surgery. Her frustration when she watched life pass me by. Mom and I had hurt side by side but never voiced our pain. I never told her I was sorry, nor did I thank her for doing for me what I couldn't do for myself.

Noletta's letter, which was actually my letter, uncorked me. Half a century of walrus tears that I had refused to cry for fear there was no happy ending, gushed out. "If only our mom could receive God's healing touch," I sobbed to my sister.

Leaving Romania, crawling up and down train steps and plane steps on my stumps and hands, enduring a ten-hour transatlantic flight, my sister and I quickly pinky-swore we would never go back. But when we asked ourselves if the trip was worth it, our hearts knew the answer. "We taught the solemn Romanians to smile; they taught us to cry," we agreed.

"And cry I did," I told a friend as I gave her my Romania recap over a cup of Starbucks coffee. I related how my mom had carried the pain of my disability to the grave and how I'd wished my mom had been in Romania to receive God's healing touch.

"Don't you think your mom has already been healed, Judy?" My friend's words stopped me short,

Mom healed? Could it be? My mind went down a path called hope. When Mom died three years earlier, she stepped into Jesus' presence. Jesus wiped away all her tears and healed her of all life's pain.

Suddenly I sensed my mom, like Noletta's, rising from her seat, walking down the aisle to me, her daughter. Their dialogue became the dialogue my mom and I had never had. And as Mom's blessing penetrated my heart, legless Judy grew wings: "Judy, you were never a burden. You were and forever will be a gift from God."

What About You?

Is there a dialogue of healing you would give anything to have? Words to fill the aching silence deep inside you? The physically broken Nolettas and Judys of this world aren't the only ones who long to be told, "You were never a burden. You were and forever will be a gift from God."

Perhaps you're a daughter but your father wanted a son. Or perhaps your single parent had to work three jobs to support you. Perhaps you disappointed your family with a pregnancy out of wedlock, or a fourth marriage, or a felony. Perhaps you were the abuser or the abused.

God, the Living Word, knows the exact words we long to hear or say, even when we don't. He can orchestrate the conversation that sets us free. Where does that bondage-breaking conversation happen? Probably tucked inside a place you'd rather not go. Possibly in a hospital's ICU or through a glass divider in the visitor's quarters at the jail. It can even happen posthumously like it did for me.

Yes, it could be painful, but oh, so worth the pain. Giving voice to a missing dialogue is one of this life's greatest gifts. Speaking or hearing words of blessing can fill the deafening silence that has tortured you your whole life. Will you give His Majesty permission to orchestrate such a dialogue? You'll be oh, so glad you did.

CHAPTER 25

His Majesty in Helplessness

If the Lord has carried you this far,
He's not going to drop you now.
You might think, "I can't make it.
I'm too weak or too wounded."
And the Lord says, "We'll make it,"
and He loads you on His back.
You might say, "My burdens are too great,"
but He carries not only your burdens but you yourself.[9]

Scott Grant

SAINT GOG'S BED AND BREAKFAST

It was our last day in Romania. Tomorrow we'd fly home. Tina and I, along with Grace and Pastor Carol, had ventured way outside our comfort zones to participate in the Becky's Hope women's retreat. Mission accomplished, we were exhausted but elated as our foursome joined the racing Romanians boarding the train to Cluj.

At age 59, I prayed I wouldn't be trampled as I, bare hands against cold metal, crawled up the steps. My sister, a young 62, followed behind lugging my wheelchair aboard. Collapsing into the nearest seat in an already full compartment, our attention was drawn out the open window to our host Lidia's wild waves. Above the roar of the engine we pieced together, "Your lodging fell through for tonight. But don't worry."

No worries mate! Our faith muscles strained yet again to trust the Lord in this foreign land. As the Romanian countryside whizzed by, my eyes fixated on a fly futilely working his way up and down the window beside me. As he labored, the following phrase kept flying around in my head:

God's greatest workshop – my helplessness!
God's greatest workshop – my helplessness!

Five hours later, we four tuckered-out Americans deboarded the train, having completed the first leg of our long journey home. Grace and Carol hustled to remove our big pile of luggage, backpacks and handbags, while Tina flexed her biceps and carried out my wheelchair. Legless Judy was the caboose, bouncing down the metal steps on her bottom with a look of *Lord, help us* plastered on her face. Like scared mice we huddled together beside the train track, watching the last of the travelers depart. Feeling deserted in a strange land, we began to wonder if Cluj, Romania had any beds with our names on them.

Finally, far in the distance we saw him. A man running toward us. His face was beet red; his hand gestures were profuse. His sputtering words contained no English. Oh dear, we'd left our translators back at the retreat center.

We deciphered that his name was Gog. He was a short,

muscular man whose smile never stopped as we made our way to the parking lot in a light rain. He led us to a little station wagon, which seemed to shrink as we surrounded it with suitcases and my wheelchair. *No way,* I thought as I looked from the car to all that needed to fit inside.

Reading my mind, he countered loudly, "No problem, no problem," in perfect English. Calmly he loaded item after item into the hatchback with just enough room on top of the luggage to slide my collapsed wheelchair. We five people fit comfortably in the front and middle.

Departing from the train station and entering into city traffic, we were stunned as our driver's hands shot skyward and he burst into song. One hymn followed another – full volume. We fluctuated between laughing, though we didn't want to be rude, and wanting to scream, "Put your hands back on the wheel," as we careened through new sights and new songs. We couldn't help but join in when we recognized the familiar-in-any-language *Battle Hymn of the Republic.*

Suddenly the car slowed and made a U turn. Bouncing on uneven dirt and gravel, we stopped in an empty corner lot, two sides of which were bordered by the street. The third side had a ten-foot tall, chain link fence, which controlled three guard dogs whose barks acknowledged our arrival. Not a house in sight.

"*Deporte,*" Gog said as he and the rest of our group opened the car doors and began to get out. I stayed put.

"Where are we going?" someone said under their breath.

"How are we going to get there?" I countered, as Gog

opened the rear of the car and began reaching for my wheelchair.

"NO! NO!" I shouted telling my sister to have him show her our destination first. He led the way. She followed with my digital camera in hand to get a picture to show me what lay ahead. Standing about 20 feet behind the car, she started laughing uncontrollably. Snapping a photo, she rushed the camera over to me. I wasn't laughing as I viewed what resembled a dry river bed with uneven rocks and broken concrete of all sizes.

The pathway to St. Gog's B&B

I sputtered sarcastically, "The path to Gog's Bed and Breakfast?" Then I started shrieking, "Hotel, Hotel," fully aware we had seen nothing resembling a hotel in the 15 minute drive from the station.

"NO, NO!" Gog was deeply hurt.

We were at an impasse. No way could a wheelchair traverse the path. Sure, in one week I'd become a pro at crawling on and off of Romanian public transportation, but no way could I make it to whatever awaited us at the end of the impassable trail. Yet no way did I want to ruin it for everyone else. Maybe I could sleep in the car? Surely the ferocious dogs would deter any troublemakers.

To this day, I don't know what broke the logjam. I think

it helped when Grace mentioned that our frustrated host had a disabled nineteen-year-old son who he carried regularly. Would I let him carry me? Any other time I would have said *Absolutely not* but it was almost 10 p.m. and we had to be at the airport in the morning by six. Tina says, "What happened next was a miraculous change of Judy's heart."

Everyone was shocked, most of all me, when I said I thought we could make it work. Gog was delighted. In a flash he squatted down beside the back seat where I was sitting. I hoisted myself up on my stumps, positioned myself as high up on his back as I could, then wrapped my arms around his neck. We were off. He walked briskly over the rock path, up two steps, through a humble kitchen and lowered me gently on to the couch. Moving to the center of the small living room, Gog's hands shot heavenward and he shouted praises to God in English, "Number One, Number One."

As a fervent prayer flowed from his heart, our hands rose upward in thanksgiving. We four collapsed onto two couches as he busily prepared a place for us. He lugged in an extra mattress, carried in a table, pulled one linen after another from the living room cupboard to make four beds. He shouted "No, No, No!" whenever we tried to help.

I didn't move from the couch for the next seven hours. Stressed to my max by the week's demands, I shut down into a protective cocoon. I could hear the conversations around me but had no energy left for the gourmet dinner consisting of little sausages, cheese and bread, served on blue and white china. As his other three guests chatted and ate, I learned later

Gog went into the bathroom. When he emerged about twenty minutes later, they realized he had been scrubbing it. Shortly before midnight, he finally excused himself to resume his 24 hour care of his severely handicapped son, Adrian.

We were awakened at five the following morning by music from a clock radio, which Gog had set the night before, anticipating that our alarm clocks were packed in our suitcases. At 5:30 on the dot he appeared at the front door holding a long-stemmed, variegated pink and yellow rose. He walked through the kitchen straight to the couch. Looking deep into my eyes, he handed me the flower calling me, "Angel. Angel." Then he stooped down so that once again I could climb on for a piggy back ride to the car.

Saint Gog and Judy

"Can you believe our week?" we said seated aboard the jumbo jet heading home to America. Reminiscing the day before aboard the train, we had been convinced that the high points had happened at the retreat center.

Gog's wife was one of the women we'd met during the week. Knowing we had to leave early to catch a plane, she volunteered her husband's services to Lidia when the other plans for our last night fell through. In response to a phone call, he had a few hours to grocery shop and ready his in-law's home for guests. He was our life-saver, arriving at the train station out of breath but with a welcome big enough for the Christ Child.

We savored the memory of this man of God whose hospitality went so far as to carry someone who couldn't go it alone on his back.

"Isn't that what God does for us?" Tina's words captured the wonder of it. We had gone to Romania to minister to moms, but at our lowest point a Romanian dad ministered to us.

"No problem! Number One!"

Gog had achieved sainthood in our books. We would forever remember Saint Gog and his life overflowing with songs of praise – full volume.

What About You?

When did God last carry you? Or haven't you let Him yet? It is a humbling experience. Being carried pricks our pride and most of us would choose to crawl instead. Only when crawling isn't an option, do we finally give in.

Funny how my life goal growing up was to become independent. That way, I'd never be a burden. Ha! God's plan is just the opposite. His greatest workshop is our helplessness. He waits for us self-sufficient humans to become dependent – first on Him, then on one another. That's the beauty of brokenness. It forces interdependence and community. Need provides a bridge one to another.

I smile when I remember Pastor Carol's response to the invitation to go along to Romania, "I'm willing to go if for no other reason than to be a sherpa to carry Judy's legs." Actually, my artificial limbs stayed home. They would have been more of a hindrance than a help. But what a declaration of love. To think someone wanted to carry my brokenness.

Actually that's what God had in mind when Jesus came to earth. Jesus, the Sherpa, came to carry us up life's mountain. He knew we couldn't make it alone. Like Saint Gog, He stoops down and invites us to climb on His back. Are you willing to let Him carry you today? His back has room enough for both of us. Jump on.

Chapter 26

His Majesty in Surrender

"Have this attitude in yourselves which was also in Christ Jesus, who although He existed in the form of God, did not regard equality with God a thing to be grasped, but emptied Himself, taking the form of a bond servant, and being made in the likeness of men. And being found in appearance as a man, He humbled Himself by becoming obedient to the point of death, even death on the cross. Therefore also God highly exalted Him..."

Philippians 2:5-9a NASB

The Good Side of Sacrifice

Pinch me. Did I, the Queen of Creature Comforts, just complete my third mission trip to Romania? I vowed I'd never go back. But God's specialty is to turn our "Not I" into "Aye, Aye Sir!" He loves breaking down our strong wills so that we can enjoy His good plan. For me, now a full-time wheelchair user, traveling to Romania spells SACRIFICE. But I'm learning that coping with inaccessible public transportation and can't-get-through-the-bathroom-door restrooms is well worth the sacrifice. That must be why I go back for more.

David and I served on the team for Joni Eareckson Tada's *Wheels for the World* wheelchair distribution in Romania in

Judy on a mission trip

2007. Our work was done in Bucharest's 100 degree summer temperatures; our lodging was alongside young adults living in an orphanage. My creature comforts included a lopsided fan, a bird chorus at dawn, a single hollyhock surviving in bone dry dirt, a nearby gas station with a wheelchair-accessible toilet, and a small plastic washtub just big enough for me to take a bath out in the courtyard.

Stripped of my air conditioned home, my three accessible toilets and my seventy rose bushes, I was able to see God's hand in my life in new ways. As I welcomed Romanian families touched by disability to the wheelchair distribution site, I saw myself: I, the disabled child, carried by a loving father. The teen, the young adult, the white haired lady – they were me too. My life flashed before me. I saw in their bleak faces my own parents, who doubted their daughter born without complete legs would ever get a life.

But wait a minute. Was it not God's bountiful blessings gushing over my six decades of life that propelled me to Romania to give back? A chill cooled my perspiring spine as I led yet another family into the Romanian church to receive a wheelchair. The mechanic, adapting each of the wheelchairs, was a stranger to them, but a husband to me. And our team's three young female physical therapists fitting the wheelchairs to the recipients were the equivalent of our three adult daughters praying for us back in America.

The good side of sacrifice is that it clears life's stage of stuff so we can see God. In Romania I saw the mighty hand of God again and again and again. Ministering to the broken, in some strange way, healed another layer of my brokenness. Nothing like a mission trip to remind me that Jesus shows up so we can face the impossible.

As our two week journey ended and our plane descended into Washington DC, my heart soared expecting all was over except the *Alleluias*. Little did I know, the trip's biggest challenge was ahead for me. After delivering 200-plus wheelchairs, my chair did not show up at the gate to greet me. It was lost at Dulles Airport. I rode in a rattle-trap airport chair to our connecting flight. I sang no *Alleluias* back in the San Francisco Bay area, when David carried me into our home or when I crawled to our bathroom that night.

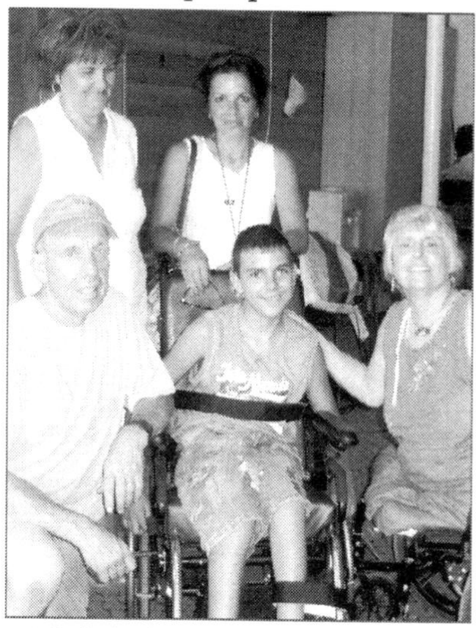

Wheels for the World trip to Romania, 2007

A battle raged within me the next morning as I steered our minivan around the airport's arrival area while David ran in to see if my wheelchair had hopefully arrived on a later flight. Each time my car approached the passenger pick-up area, I heard a still small voice, *Am I enough?*

Stubbornly I argued, "God, You know I need my wheelchair. You know Judy can't do life without wheels!" My eyes searched eagerly for David, each time I made the loop. Hopefully he would have my chair.

Am I enough?

Approaching now the seventh time, through tears I could see David standing alone. Finally my will broke, surrendering to a God, who promises a plan that is always good. "OK, Lord, You are enough," I blubbered.

Steering our minivan toward the curb, I then saw it on the far side of David – MY wheelchair.

Once my chair and I were reunited, I could relax and see God's hand even in this. Early on, I had prayed for goose bump stories from Romania. I got not only goose bumps but a chill when I pondered the paradox of my lost wheelchair. Ironically, I had delivered wheelchairs so no one would need to crawl and in the end, I was forced to crawl.

Does no good deed go unpunished? Or is there a lesson here? I realize now my going to Romania was a sacrifice. But the supreme sacrifice is not one that you or I engineer. It's a moment by moment acceptance of the Heavenly Father's will; it's putting our strong wills on the altar as a sacrifice and abandoning ourselves to His good plan even when it feels bad. I, as a human being, fall far short of that. That's why I join the angels in applauding Jesus as the King of Sacrifice.

WHAT ABOUT YOU?

How often have you thought, "No good deed goes unpunished?" What account can you give of an act of kindness that wrought suffering in your life? Parenting may surely qualify when our kids display an attitude of entitlement in place of gratitude. Or what about the driver who stops to help a traveler in distress and in so doing becomes permanently maimed by a passing semi? Or the widow whose husband forfeits His life to save a drowning child?

Am I enough? asks the still small voice. *Am I enough?*
Have you heard His Majesty asking you, *Am I enough?*

I love the prayer found on the body of a Southern soldier during the Civil War. His words shout, "Yes, Lord, You are enough." His life and death convey, "No matter what's missing, God is enough."

Confederate Soldier's Prayer

I asked God for strength, that I might achieve,
I was made weak, that I might learn humbly to obey.
I asked God for health, that I might do greater things,
I was given infirmity, that I might do better things.
I asked for riches, that I might be happy,
I was given poverty, that I might be wise.
I asked for power, that I might have the praise of men,

I was given weakness, that I might feel the need of God.
I asked for all things, that I might enjoy life,
I was given life, that I might enjoy all things.
I got nothing that I asked for
but everything I had hoped for.
Almost despite myself,
my unspoken prayers were answered.
I am among men, most richly blessed.[10]

Chapter 27
His Majesty in Darkness

God takes the people who have been cast aside,
who look like trash.
He's in the recycling business.
He recycles that trash and brings forth a treasure.
Paula White

The Reward at Midnight

It was the last day of our Joni and Friends wheelchair distribution in Brazil. We were all exhausted. Friday's work had begun at 9 a.m. It was almost midnight. We'd been at it for 15 hours. Over 150 times during the week our *Wheels for the World* team members had performed the exercise – welcoming a family, gathering information, assigning a physical therapist and a mechanic to take measurements, selecting and modifying a wheelchair, and for many customizing a seat cushion, a head support, or seat belt. All of this from start to finish was wrapped in the good news of Jesus Christ, the ultimate Healer. Often I acted as a greeter welcoming the families with, "The wheelchair you will receive is a gift from Jesus." But the crowning touch was when the evangelists presented the plan of salvation producing a harvest of ninety-three individuals born into the family of God.

Our hearts vacillated between amazement at what God had done and jubilation that we were near the finish line. Co-laboring beside Brazilian mechanics, therapists, plus the dedicated-to-the-cause Rotary Club members and our interpreters, we had all worked hard without complaint. In four days time, 151 wheelchairs were given out with today's tally alone being a record-breaking 51.

By early morning the waiting area had filled to capacity. Family after family – some had arrived at 8 a.m. – sat in silence waiting their turn for the miracle of mobility. Their not-sure-what-to-expect, expressionless faces lit up with hope as they were singled out of the crowd. A man, who two years earlier had fallen from scaffolding, arrived on a gurney accompanied by a devoted wife, his sole caregiver. A dozen white-haired men and women sat lined up against one wall. They'd be easy to fit with an adult wheelchair, a two-inch cushion and a seat belt. It was the children and adults with twisted bodies, who provided the greatest challenge. Customizing a chair could take one seating specialist most of a day.

Our hearts warmed as we witnessed the dedication of mothers cradling their disabled children as Mary cradled the Christ Child. Our watches read 6 p.m. as we assured each other – surely no more recipients would come. At that instant, six more families arrived. Our leader called the team to a circle of prayer, as was his custom in times of trouble. Together we held hands and prayed for God's resurrection power to enable us to finish the course.

Therapists and mechanics focused only on the person in front of them, afraid to guess how many were yet to be seen. One at a time, the masses were given a wheelchair – a chair that had been prayed over and even anointed with olive oil the day it arrived. We worked steadily into the night. Finally at 11:30 only three families remained, each situated around their severely disabled loved one who lay comfortably on a thin green rubber mat inside the fitting area.

It was almost midnight – five minutes to twelve – when I noticed a gaunt, stiff-as-a-board figure on the mat. Wheelchair Recipient Number 151. *He had no stately form or majesty that I should look upon him. Surely he was a man of sorrows acquainted with grief.* Isaiah 52:2-3 NASB His helplessness, his brokenness drew me in. Suddenly I sensed the unthinkable – *It's Jesus. It's Jesus in disguise.* First I told Matt, the physical therapist who had just given a thumbs up – the wheelchair was ready. Like the Little Red Hen who shouted, *the sky is falling,* I announced to everyone in the room, *Jesus is here.*

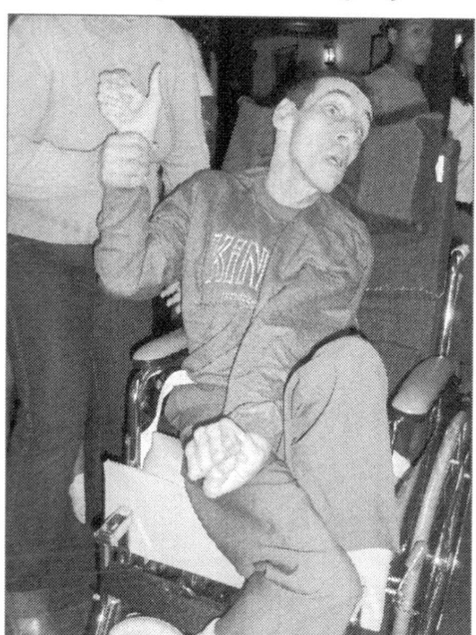

Wheelchair Recipient 151, Brazil, 2008

It's Jesus in disguise.

As three team members gently lifted the fifty year old man, who was crippled from birth, into his first-in-his-life wheelchair, our work site became holy ground. Our team leader choked up, as he thanked the family for the privilege of serving them. Another team member prayed and praised the holy name of God, whose only begotten Son became handicapped in our place. And as the clock struck midnight, our team who had given and given all week became the recipients of a holy thank you as our last wheelchair recipient moved his lips ever so slightly, and blessed us with what his family described was a kiss.

As the family exited, my wheelchair and I followed them out the door into the darkness. Raucous music intruded upon the sacredness of the moment as a band entertained 1300 guests in the club's ballroom nearby. And even from the distribution room, I could hear our team break forth into a jubilant "Happy Birthday" as Greg, our fearless, faith-filled leader turned 50 years young.

Too quickly I would be swept up by the temporal. Yes, life would return to normal, but my life would never be the same. I had seen Jesus. True to His style, He had not come atop a white stallion, but humbled himself as on a donkey. Jesus had shown up, not as the Commodore of the Clube Naval, where we had distributed wheelchairs all week, but in a mute, gnarled figure on the floor. God's Lamb without defect had come in bodily form to take upon Himself the defects of mankind.

What About You?

Have you seen Him yet? I waited for 63 years before I actually saw Him. Yes, I'd seen glimpses of Him in the faces of broken children and battle-weary adults and yes, I'd learned to look for Him on duty in my places of brokenness but this time I saw His gnarled body.

I do agree gnarled bodies take some getting used to. I remember the afternoon I drove a van load of kindergartners to take cookies to the severely disabled kids at Green Pastures group home. When Brandon and his gnarled body welcomed them at the door, they scurried like scared mice into the van. Too often we humans don't get it no matter what age we are.

And yet the Son of God gives us a clue where He resides. His life-changing interactions were with lepers, the demon possessed, paralytics, the blind and broken – all of whom, thanks to their crushed condition, knew they needed a Savior. Maybe it's time to thank God for whatever it is that handicaps our proud self-sufficiency so that we can see and receive Him. Maybe it's time to hand over our disdain for imperfections in others and ourselves – to see disfigurement for what it really is – His Majesty's castle here on earth.

Lord, we give You permission to produce the paradigm shift required so that we don't remain ignorant. Give us eyes to see. We don't want to miss You in all Your glory today!

Chapter 28
His Majesty in the Winter of Life

I will be your God through all your lifetime,
yes, even when your hair is white with age.
I made you and I will care for you.
I will carry you along and be your Savior.

Isaiah 46:4 TLB

The Old Lady with No Legs

I – by now a seasoned senior citizen – was finishing up my grocery shopping at Walmart near our home in southern Oregon when I overheard his remark. Turning in the direction of the voice I saw a little boy, maybe five-years-old. Obviously he saw me as he announced to his mother, "Look at the old lady with no legs."

A warm smile filled my innards lighting up my face. Surprisingly I wasn't downed by the all-too-familiar cloud of shame similar words would have brought in the past. Actually I kind of liked the name, *The Old Lady with No Legs*. I repeated it to myself again and again throughout the day. Was I finally becoming comfortable in my own skin?

It was about six months later that my granddaughter, Brianna and I were in the Kids Zone at our local athletic club. Just the two of us in a fenced-in area while her mama and daddy worked out. *What fun to be a Grandma.* Feeling safe, I climbed out of my wheelchair to join grandbaby on the carpeted floor. For a one-year-old, this toy-filled area surely equaled a day at Disneyland.

Granddaughter Brianna and Granny Goose Judy

Savoring the moment, I leaned back studying the unending labyrinth of plastic tubing above us for older children to crawl through. That's when I saw them above us, two girls, maybe six and eight-years-old, with their noses pinned against the tubing's plastic window. Instantly my defenses went into high alert.

Their chant tortured me. Obviously they had spotted my disability: "Stand up! Stand up! Stand up!" became "Where are your legs? Where are your legs?"

At first I tried to ignore them, but their annoying remarks continued. Finally I shouted, "Go away!" Instead they came closer. No longer peering through the climbing structure, they popped up on the other side of the five-foot tall fence, jumping up and gawking in. *What to do?*

I didn't hear him arrive but suddenly my son-in-law, Beau, stood not too far from them. He'd come back early to check on us, he said, but my version was he was sent by God. His six-foot height instantly tipped the scale. The girls made a quick departure and trapped Judy was safe.

Daughter Elizabeth arrived a few minutes later. Instantly she shared my frustration offering loving words of comfort, "Mom, you are so strong yet so vulnerable."

Of course she understood. As a child, she or one of her sisters were my scouts at the swim club. They'd run ahead to check out the terrain, and then come back to the car to let me know whether the coast was clear. Only if the pool were kid-free, would I come out for my swim. Funny how some things never change. As life would have it, even innocent children can become predators when they taste power over the powerless.

It was the next morning. I was a member of a planning team for an upcoming Joni and Friends Family Retreat in Oregon. The retreats are designed to provide spiritual and emotional support for families coping with discrimination and exclusion due to disability. Seated around our meeting tables were seasoned veterans of the disabled world, themselves or a family member living with physical, mental, emotional and or social limitations.

What a perfect place to ask for counsel about the trauma the day before. Surely this group would understand and provide the wisdom I craved. No one stirred as I told my story, my voice filled with emotion, my tear ducts plugged with tears I couldn't cry. The first to respond to my request for counsel was a mom with a young adult son born with spina bifida. "Education works well for our family, Judy," she said as she handed us each a flyer that she and her son had created with his photo and a brief life story inside. She told of his experience one day at the library, similar to mine but with a different ending. The informative brochure had succeeded in transforming two harassing little girls into his best friends.

Another group member – donning a scar on his head from a bullet wound and a below the knee prosthesis from a motorcycle accident – said humor was his ticket. To a curiosity seeker's question, "Where's your leg?" he very well might playfully growl back, "A shark bit it off!" His young wife seated beside him then told how love and lots of patience had brought understanding to their friend who had been insensitive toward their son with Down syndrome.

I listened eagerly wanting so much for my two-ton weight to be lifted. But my heaviness persisted even when the woman across from me, a thyroid cancer survivor, said she knew my life to be a great encouragement to others having heard my keynote speech at a recent luncheon.

As we broke for lunch, I thought the feedback was over. To be honest I was disappointed that none of the comments brought the understanding I longed for. That's when God Himself gave me His thoughts, setting my spirit free: *Education and humor are super and I use them in others, Judy, but where I feel most at home in you is in your brokenness. We're writing a story about brokenness, remember? Write this story down to give courage to others to embrace their brokenness.*

Finally comforted, my mind and now calmed heart revisited my scene of humiliation the day before. Was somebody else inside the Kid's Zone-turned-torture-chamber? My memory scanned the corner shelves overflowing with happy toys every toddler would love. I remembered the labyrinth of plastic tubing. Again I saw two scrunched faces straining to see my brokenness. Then my mind's eye came to rest on the cushioned rocker in the middle of the room. Someone was in it. Then I saw Him, the Man of Sorrows, acquainted with grief. He was weeping.

How easy it would be to beat myself up for going down for the count with the little girls at the Kids Zone. But wait a minute. Did I? Looking back I see that something monumental happened. Within 24 hours I saw Jesus on the scene with me. Twenty four hours versus the half a century required before I saw Him with me at Shriners Hospital and during my lonely teen years. Seeing His Majesty on the scene transformed my place of humiliation into holy ground. Higher ground. The good news: Short, midget-sized Judy Ann is standing taller and taller, gaining new heights every day.

I add my voice to my friend Sam Bloomer's favorite song, the song of his heart that rang loud and clear even after Alzheimer's had silenced his baritone voice. My faith has caught the joyful sound of Sam's voice from the grandstands of heaven where those who could not speak will shout and sing:

Higher Ground

Johnson Oatman, Jr.

I'm pressing on the upward way,
New heights I'm gaining every day;
Still praying as I'm onward bound,
Lord, plant my feet on higher ground.

My heart has no desire to stay
Where doubts arise and fears dismay;
Tho' some may dwell where these abound,
My prayer, my aim is higher ground.

I want to live above the world,
Though Satan's darts at me are hurled;
For faith has caught the joyful sound,
The song of saints on higher ground.

I want to scale the utmost height
And catch a gleam of glory bright;
But still I'll pray till heav'n I've found,
Lord, lead me on to higher ground.

CHORUS

Lord, lift me up and let me stand
By faith, on heaven's table-land,
A higher plane than I have found;
Lord, plant my feet on higher ground.[11]

WHAT ABOUT YOU?

Have shame or pain drowned out the song in your life? Are you deflated or defeated? Have doubts and fears knocked you off your feet? Has your last hope died on the vine?

Listen up. Can you hear it? The song of the ages – the joyful song of the saints on higher ground? Can you make out what they're saying? They're exhorting you to:

- Embrace your brokenness.
- Find the Man of Sorrows waiting for you there.
- Take hold of His nail-scarred hand.
- Appropriate His power made perfect in your weakness.

Can you add your voice to the song of those saints? The only requirement is you must be broken in one way or another. Dig deep in the rubble and unearth God's gold, His treasure hewn out of your brokenness. Leave your shame at His nail-scarred feet and walk forth with dignity. Consider yourself a work-in-progress as His Majesty unveils His Masterpiece in you.

Chapter 29
His Majesty in Brokenness

"My grace is enough; it's all you need.
My strength comes into its own in your weakness."
Once I heard that, I was glad to let it happen.
I quit focusing on the handicap and began appreciating the gift.
It was a case of Christ's strength moving in on my weakness.
Now I take limitations in stride, and with good cheer,
these limitations that cut me down to size –
abuse, accidents, opposition, bad breaks.
I just let Christ take over!
And so the weaker I get, the stronger I become.

II Corinthians 12:9-10 MSG

When It Can't Be Fixed

I was a fairly new Christian when I came upon Paul's thorny dilemma in II Corinthians 12, where he sought relief from suffering but received something better. In the middle of my college career, looking forward to summer school with my new beau David Squier, I ended up instead on an operating table. Like Paul, three times I asked the Lord for a quick fix but instead I underwent arm surgery for a troubled ulnar nerve and spent the summer back at home convalescing.

We don't know what Paul's thorn was but anyone who has

suffered needs to know what Paul's take away was. In place of physical healing, God Himself comforted him with a spiritual treatise that would make any one of us willing to suffer: *My grace is enough; it's all you need. My strength comes into its own in your weakness.* II Corinthians 12:9a MSG

God got a lot of mileage out of Paul's thorn. Thanks to it, the mystery of brokenness is unveiled: weakness need not make us weaker. Actually weakness can open the floodgates for His strength, and as impossible as it may seem the weaker I get, the stronger I can become.

The truth is, we can believe something with our heads but our hearts aren't quite there yet. I must admit I've become envious talking to able-bodied friends and family members temporarily disabled with a broken leg or arm. I know the sequence: they struggle to manage the new normal; they endure the inconvenience for several weeks or months and then *presto,* they trade their cast and crutches for their mountain bike or tennis racket. *They're the lucky duckies,* I can't help but think.

What does one do when it doesn't go away? Like Joni or Renee Bondi, both of them paralyzed from the neck down? No longer able to jump out of bed in the morning or get dressed or undressed alone or walk on the beach hand in hand with their husbands. What keeps them going?

Then there's Dave Dravecky, a former pitcher with the San Francisco Giants, who lived through the unthinkable – cancer in his pitching arm. Dave's glorious book *Comeback,* documenting his miraculous return to the game, was soon to be followed by *When You Can't Come Back.* What does a body do when your golden arm is cut off into the shoulder, taking with it your lifelong dream, your career, your livelihood, your identity, your dignity?

What about a parent facing the reality of a permanently disabled child? Knowing, as my parents did, that short of a creative miracle, my legs wouldn't grow and my left hand wouldn't work. How does a parent cope with the reality of a child born with cerebral palsy or Down syndrome? Or even the death of a child? What do you do when the problem in yourself or a loved one is permanent and can't be fixed? When kiss and make it better doesn't make it better. When medical technology and a "can do" attitude won't fix it. How can we cope when there is no hope?

One evening, I wheeled out of the women's dressing room at our neighborhood swim club into a conversation between another member and the club's custodian. The troubled mom was nursing her aching back in the steaming hot tub. I stopped in my tracks as I heard the hymn-humming custodian's testimonial: "Our faith determines the outcome. I prayed without ceasing about my back problem. I believed God's promises. Now look at me, I'm healed."

Sitting legless in my wheelchair, ready to jump into the pool, I jumped instead into the conversation. Flinging my arms heavenward, I looked the man's insensitivity in the eye and blubbered, "When God doesn't heal us, He inhabits us!"

That's my goal in this life called Christian – Jesus in me and I in Him. But how do we get there? I believe the interchange happens when our suffering whittles down our self-sufficiency and independence so that the only choice remaining becomes everything from God, nothing from me.

Based on the truth that I know, this old lady with no legs has made peace with my Creator's creation called Judy. Pivotal to that peace is the reality that, *You were there while I was being formed in utter seclusion! You saw me before I was born...* Psalm 139:15-16a TLB

As strange as it may sound, I tell people His Majesty and I met in utero when He put His stake in the ground and assured me that my birth defect was not a fetal fluke but holy design. His Majesty showing up in my brokenness makes it all worthwhile.

Judy on her 60th birthday

What About You?

Have you made peace with how God made you? Not just how He made your mind and body, but the family and culture you were born into? And what about the skills He's given or not given you? Have you made peace with the unfixable brokenness in your life or that of a loved one?

He is the Mastermind over all of His creation. His fingerprints are everywhere. Even something as basic as our name fits into His Master Plan.

I was enjoying my morning devotions on my 50th birthday when out of the blue I began to wrestle with God about my birth defect:

> Judy: "What a dirty trick, Lord, creating me without complete legs!"
> God: *I had My foot in the door when your mom chose the name Judy.*
> Judy: "Your foot in the door, Lord?"
> God: *Yes, I had My foot in the door for praise. Your mom didn't know it, but Judy means praise.*
> Judy: "Who needs legs when God's foot is on the scene?"

His Majesty sees His finished work in us long before our

knocking knees get there. He's got His foot in the door of your brokenness just like He did for mine. Can you begin by handing over what you call your flaws so that you can find peace in His holy design?

My prayer for you is two fold: that you would find His Masterpiece in your missing piece and His Master's Peace in your missing peace. To think God has an unexpected fix all figured out for what appears unfixable in your life.

Can you embrace who you are and how He's made you? Take a deep breath before the plunge. Then surrender your brokenness to His Majesty. *Now may the Lord of peace Himself continually grant you peace in every circumstance. The Lord be with you all!* II Thessalonians 3:16 NASB

Chapter 30
His Majesty in the Unthinkable

He came to die on a piece of wood,
but made the hill on which it stood.

Author Unknown

The Wonderful Cross

"You really want me to trace my hand inside the front cover of your Bible?"

I looked at my deformed hand and back at Kristin, remembering how I'd nicknamed her Christ-in twenty years earlier when we began our weekly Moms In Touch[12] prayer times together. She and I had carried many prayer concerns to the cross, some answers to which were recorded on the pages of my Bible. Now she was going a step further, wanting me to trace my three-fingered hand in her holy book.

It was obvious she wasn't backing down as she opened her Bible and handed me a pen. My hesitation was quickly replaced by a heart that was willing as I realized this unlovely left hand had been a master at teaching me kingdom lessons.

Kristin watched as I traced around a normal-looking thumb, a towering middle finger and a crooked, scarred pinky.

Carefully, I recorded a few words inside each finger, representing my three point sermon, which had popped up five years earlier in Romania when my hand popped out of hiding:

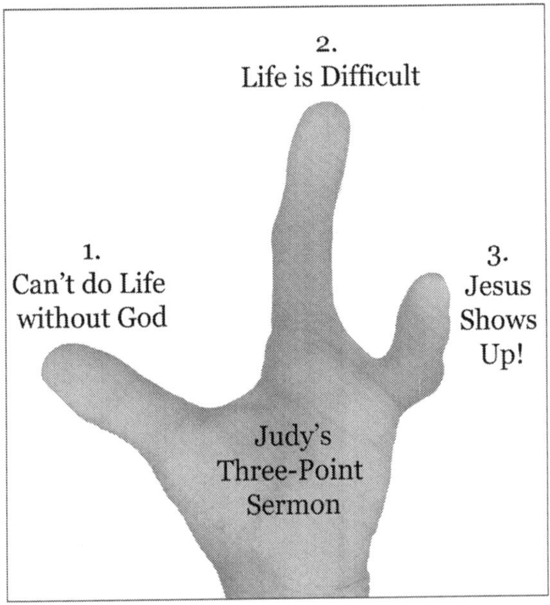

I looked from the drawing now in Kristin's Bible to my flesh and bones and realized though many people don't notice my deformity, not a day had gone by that my left-handed brokenness hadn't stared me in the face. Hadn't three fingers forced a Plan B when David blessed me with a diamond? With my left hand at my side, I'd announce my engagement to friends explaining that I, like the Europeans, wore my ring on my right hand. For the big day, my family adapted my pearl-sequined wedding gloves by sticking cotton balls where two fingers were supposed to be. And, truth be told, my left hand had embarrassed me more than once when an unsuspecting child grew squeamish about holding it.

Experiences like that kept my consciousness on the alert, but one day my hand and I were laid low by an inner disconnect I knew nothing about. During a weekly counseling session, in an effort to better process my life's experiences, my counselor asked a seemingly innocuous question, "Is there anything adult Judy would like to say to little Judy?"

Like a cannon-ball, my words shook the room: "I don't want to talk to her. She's a freak!"

Seeking to provide comfort the counselor moved her chair closer placing her hand on my arm. Relief was out of reach until suddenly, as if they had a mind of their own, my five fingers on my intact hand reached across the battle line inside me to provide a protective shield over its disfigured partner. Deep down, all the way to the bottom of my stumps, I suddenly felt safe, loved, and cared for. Wholeness embraced brokenness. Brokenness received relief. Shame vanished.

My memories stepped aside as I handed Kristin her Bible. Together we pondered the depths of His Majesty's unthinkable masterpiece – my disfigurement His instrument of choice to make Judy His *visual aid to demonstrate who He really is...*" (See Joni Eareckson Tada quote, page 1).

The minute Kristin left I realized I had an unscheduled appointment with my own Bible to make an addition. With a new affection, thanks to my friend, I placed my hand center-page and traced a one-of-a-kind handprint on the inside of the cover. It was then that I saw it – for the first time – my hand's outline resembled a cross. A cross that whispered, *Your suffering will not be wasted. Trust Me. I'll take care of the hard part. Remember, don't quit before the happy ending.*

To think it had stared me in the face everyday of my life for 65 years and I just now saw it. To think it had been there as my eight fingers pecked out hymns on Dad's old piano half a century earlier:

The Old Rugged Cross

George Bennard

On a hill far away stood an old rugged cross,
The emblem of suff'ring and shame;
And I love that old cross where the dearest and best
For a world of lost sinners was slain.

Refrain:
So I'll cherish the old rugged cross,
'Til my trophies at last I lay down;
I will cling to the old rugged cross,
And exchange it some day for a crown.

Oh, that old rugged cross, so despised by the world,
Has a wondrous attraction for me;
For the dear Lamb of God left His glory above
To bear it to dark Calvary.

In that old rugged cross, stained with blood so divine,

A wondrous beauty I see,
For 'twas on that old cross Jesus suffered and died,
To pardon and sanctify me.

To the old rugged cross I will ever be true;
Its shame and reproach gladly bear;
Then He'll call me some day to my home far away,
Where His glory forever I'll share.[13]

Christ the Redeemer watching over Rio de Janeiro, Brazil

The truth is the cross can be the healer-of-life's-wounds to some of us but sickeningly bitter and repulsive to others. Nailed to the cross Jesus was smack dab in the middle of two worldviews. One criminal hurled abuse at Him: "Are you not the Christ? Save Yourself and save us!" But the other's words surely gave proof that His crucifixion was worth all the pain: "Jesus, remember me when you come in Your kingdom." (See Luke 23:39-43 NASB) That second criminal's very words hit the nail on the head. Indeed, Christ came so that humanity could once again call His kingdom their Home.

And the road Home is none other than the road of suffering. On that road we meet a Fellow-traveler bearing eternal scars in His hands, proof of a battle won long ago on our behalf on an old rugged cross. He's committed to journeying with us, whether invited or not. And safely Home we will experience what eluded us here on earth, what is now ours, thanks to His Majesty, the Son of God's divine appointment with the cross. *He shall wipe away every tear from their eyes; and there shall no longer be any death; there shall no longer be any mourning, or crying or pain...* Revelation 21:4 NASB

Winding this book up, I remembered my son-in-law Beau's question a year earlier: "What's your brand, Judy? What's your brand?"

At the time I hemmed and hawed, clarity eluding me. But today, my dear Son-in-law, I know the answer: "My brand is my disfigured hand, a daily reminder that those who seek will find the cross of Christ in their suffering. The goal in this life is finding Him. And when we find Him, we will say like St Augustine, *In my deepest wound I saw His glory, and it dazzled me."*

WHAT ABOUT YOU?

Have you found the cross of Christ in your brokenness? It's there, I'm convinced. Don't expect to find it in the attic with your sports trophies, or on the wall with your diplomas, or in your jewelry box with your retirement watch. Look for the cross in the rubble of your life.

What is killing you? Your declining health? Poverty? Humiliation? Family conflict? Grief? Torment? Disappointment? Fear of death? Whatever your rubble may be, His Majesty's promise from the old rugged cross is: *I am the resurrection and the life; he who believes in Me shall live even if he dies, and everyone who lives and believes in Me shall never die. Do you believe this?* John 11:25-26 NASB

And from the wonderful cross, His Majesty extends this too-good-to-be-true invitation: Hand over your handicaps. Bring me your wheelchairs. Your empty chairs. Your size 4X shirt. Your unresolved conflict. Your bankruptcy papers. Your tear-filled hankies. Your shame. Your aging body. Your stumbling block of can-do pride. And your sense of unworthiness. I've taken care of all of it. The battle's won. The debt has been paid in full.

What does the cross say to you? Maybe it leaves you cold. I pray His love will warm you. Maybe it's an enigma. You say, "Suffering ain't what I signed up for!" Maybe you, like I, still have much to learn from it. The good news is His Majesty meets us wherever we are. At the top of His list is not condemnation, but love – love that seeks us every day of our lives. The cross is proof of that. The truth is, nails didn't hold the Son of God to the old rugged cross. Love did.

I asked Jesus, "How much do you love me?"
He answered, "This much,"
and stretched out His arms and died.

Author Unknown

End Notes

1 Used by permission from Joni Eareckson Tada, Joni and Friends International Disability Center, All rights reserved.

2 *Star Light, Star Bright,* Public Domain.

3 Edgar Guest, *It Couldn't Be Done,* Public Domain.

4 John Ortberg, Big God/Little God sermon series, *God is Big Enough,* October 28, 2007.

5 Max Lucado, *A Gentle Thunder* (Nashville:Thomas Nelson, Inc., 1995), 122.

6 Ruth Harms Calkin, *Keep Me Faithful* (Wheaton, Illinois: Tyndale House Publishers, Inc., 1996), 119.

7 Annie Johnson Flint, *He Giveth More Grace,* Public Domain.

8 Used by permission from Ruth Harms Calkin, *My God is So Big,* All rights reserved.

9 Scott Grant, *The God Who Carries You,* http://www.pbc.org/messages/10562.

10 *Confederate Soldier's Prayer,* Public Domain.

11 Johnson Oatman, Jr., Higher Ground, Public Domain.

12 www.momsintouch.org

13 George Bennard, *The Old Rugged Cross,* Public Domain.

Made in the USA
Charleston, SC
17 May 2011